THE FLAVOUR OF SCOTLAND

THE BEST OF SCOTTISH COOKING

Edited by
Brian Hannan

IN ASSOCIATION WITH
THE SCOTTISH CHEFS ASSOCIATION

MAINSTREAM
PUBLISHING

EDINBURGH AND LONDON

First published in Great Britain in 1995 by
MAINSTREAM PUBLISHING COMPANY (EDINBURGH) LTD
7 Albany Street
Edinburgh EH1 3UG

ISBN 1 85158 725 X

A catalogue record for this book is available from the British Library

Typeset in Garamond by Litho Link Ltd, Welshpool, Powys
Printed and bound in Great Britain by BPC Hazell Books Ltd, Aylesbury

CONTENTS

INTRODUCTION

SCOTLAND'S CULINARY MIRACLE

SCOTLAND has been famous for its food for hundreds of years. Everyone knows that Scotland produces venison, salmon, trout, pheasant, lobsters, scallops, mussels, cod, cheese, honey, mushrooms, turnip, lentils, pork, beef, lamb, potatoes and haddock. But it is only in the last decade that its cooking has caught up. And in that short time, Scotland has achieved a culinary miracle. From being the genuine no-hopers of European cuisine, Scottish chefs have achieved a dramatic renaissance, and now Scotland has more Michelin-starred chefs per capita than anywhere else in the UK.

Despite this outstanding achievement, the true quality of Scottish cooking has never been fully recognised. Part of the reason lies in the fact that no one really knows what Scottish cooking is. We all know it's not haggis and neeps, nor is it anything to do with thistles and mists and kilts, and it is a million miles from the culinary myths so enticingly marketed by the Burns and Hogmanay industries. Yet its true character is not so hard to find – you only have to look. In fact, any country's cooking is defined by its top practitioners. If the Scottish style has been undiscovered, it has a lot to do with the lack of serious attention given to serious Scottish cooking and with the lack of a comprehensive guide to the best in Scottish cooking. This book, at last, will provide a basic understanding of the new Scottish cooking style, of what is really happening.

Scottish cooking is rooted in Scottish produce. Of that there is no doubt. But those roots have sometimes seemed like immovable chains. For the one thing the chefs represented in this book have done is free Scotland from the bad cooking done to its good produce – to remove salmon from the shackles of dry grilling, to rescue pigeon from the prison of overcooking. Scotland's great chefs have shown that, in many cases, the greatest service you can do to Scottish produce is to undercook it, to treat it lightly, for the full flavour needs only a little room to breathe, and certainly does not need to be smothered. The best Scottish cooking is defined by flavour not presentation. Pretty pictures on a plate have never been

11

the Scottish culinary style. The great dark flavours of Scotland – our venison, our meats, lentils, broth, stews, pigeon – just get in the way.

The extraordinary thing about Scottish cooking is that it has been reinvented over the last two decades. That there has been a revolution in cooking and cooking style is beyond question. The renaissance began in an apparently unpromising location which had been taken over by a man with no formal culinary training. But when David Wilson opened the Peat Inn on one of Fife's many blasted heaths in 1972, he could not have foreseen that he would become a figurehead for a new generation of chefs. Over the next few years, as if by magic, three other people with little or no formal training were also setting up shop. Hilary Brown, in equally unprepossessing premises, started cooking at La Potiniere in Gullane, Ronnie Clydesdale was setting up in a back alley in Glasgow's west end under the guise of the Ubiquitous Chip, and Betty Allen was starting off at Airds Hotel in Port Appin, Argyll.

The 1980s saw a further fluttering of talent – Jim Graham at Ostler's Close in Fife, Ferrier Richardson at October in Glasgow, Jim Kerr at the Rogano, Nick Nairn at Braeval Old Mill in Aberfoyle. For a time Perthshire seemed awash with top chefs – Bruce Sangster at Murrayshall House, Frances Atkins at Farleyer House and John Webber at Kinnaird.

In 1990 Scotland had two Michelin-starred restaurants. In 1991 it had six, including the Peat Inn, Braeval Old Mill, Airds, and La Potiniere. It was an astonishing jump in standards. The 1990s could see even more growth in quality. Andrew Radford has found a restaurant to match his talent in The Atrium in Edinburgh, and last year Keith and Nicola Braidwood, both under 30, opened up their eponymous restaurant in Dalry in Ayrshire.

It has been a slow simmer, but one of the great joys of eating around Scotland is that so many of the top chefs do not reside in the big cities. So for a tourist, the end of a city's boundaries do not signal the end of good eating. Top chefs have been planted all over Scotland, mostly in small towns and villages. There is a reason for this. When chefs like David Wilson and Hilary Brown started out, their main aim was to find somewhere they could afford, and that ruled out most of the city centres.

As in France, the best Scottish chefs are chef-proprietors. They have done their learning and their growing, by and large, in one restaurant. They cannot easily uproot themselves and go. They have become synonymous with certain places. They have proven that if you are good, if you are better, the discerning diner will find you.

The other extraordinary fact about many of Scotland's top chefs is that they are self-taught. Hilary Brown went straight from college to her own restaurant, David Wilson was in marketing, Nick Nairn was in the Merchant Navy, Andrew Radford was an assistant hotel manager, and Ronnie Clydesdale worked in the whisky business. But while they all caught the bug, they never fell prey to the mystique. They cooked it as they saw it.

Some of Scotland's top chefs aren't Scottish at all. Frances Atkins and John Webber left succesful businesses down south to come to Scotland for the quality of life and the quality and range of fresh produce. And a lot of Scotland's top chefs are women, a greater proportion than anywhere else in Britain.

Here at last is a taste of the great chefs of Scotland, offering a range of inspiring and easy recipes, turning their great beam of talent on to everything, from the humble cod to lobster, from duck to courgette filo-pastry flan. Each chef has contributed a number of their favourite recipes. From starters to main courses and desserts, here is an opportunity to wallow in some of the best recipes in the country. From simple, hearty fare to more sophisticated dishes, there are fabulous easy-to-make soups, terrines, vegetarian and traditional dishes, an entire spectrum of exciting cooking. Perhaps the most underrated part of Scottish cuisine is its puddings, ice-creams, gratins, parfaits, chocolate desserts, meringues, mousses, truffles, all the great favourites with a Scottish twist.

Everyone has different ideas. Hilary Brown cooks her salmon on spicy lentils, while David Wilson prefers using Szechuan peppercorns and celeriac purée. Jim Graham likes his salmon with a salt crust and spicy cabbage with a butter sauce, while John Webber opts for apple and basil and a light vegetable dressing. For some, salmon isn't king. Ronnie Clydesdale cooks halibut in a pine-kernel-and-green-peppercorn crust with red-wine-and-chocolate sauce, while Frances Atkins goes for Mediterranean fish with roast vegetables and Thai sauce, and Nick Nairn reminds us of how wonderful cod can be served with mash and spring onion and chives. And there are recipes for sole and haddock, sea-bass and red mullet, and halibut and turbot.

And Scotland's great wealth of game produce is well served with recipes for guinea-fowl, duck, pigeon, hare, venison, grouse and pheasant. There are umpteen recipes for seafood and beef, and lamb and soup and pasta and on and on.

This is a book of secrets, too. Hilary Brown and Nick Nairn tell you the secret of how to make wonderful soups, David Wilson reveals how to make the 'ultimate' caramel pudding, and John Webber astonishes with his courgette filo pastry. It's also a book of surprises – you will discover why poaching beef is good for you and how to make perfect truffles.

Scottish produce lends itself particularly well to vegetarian dishes. There are a number of designated recipes as well as many which can be cooked aside from the dish which they accompany.

This is a book whose time has come. The best of Scotland's chefs cooking the best Scottish dishes using the best Scottish produce. I hope you enjoy it.

Brian Hannan, editor

THE SCOTTISH CHEFS ASSOCIATION

The Scottish Chefs Association is unique in its aims and ambitions. Less than two years old, it already has over 150 members from all over Scotland – from Shetland and Orkney to the main cities and the Borders.

It was set up as an educational initiative and to promote the overall excellence of Scottish culinary talent. This book is tangible evidence that the Scottish Chefs Association is fulfilling its role to provide a wider platform for the growing excellence of Scottish cooking.

Less obvious has been the success of its educational operation. The Scottish Chefs Association organises over 25 one-day training workshops and educational dinners every year for its members. These are held in working restaurants rather than lecture theatres and provide the opportunity for younger and older chefs to have access to the best culinary brains in the country.

You may be astonished to discover that this level of commitment by top chefs to help train other chefs does not exist anywhere else in Britain. The workshops and dinners are hosted by the chefs featured in this book and others. All the chefs hosting these activities are giving up their time to do so. These top chefs have committed their time to the Scottish Chefs Association because they believe it is the only way forward, to continue improving standards and to bring together the best in Scottish cooking.

The Scottish Chefs Association is sponsored by Booker Fitch and Scottish Enterprise.

The Organiser of the Scottish Chefs Association is Brian Hannan. The Advisory Board comprises Betty Allen, Hilary Brown, David Wilson, Nick Nairn, Frances Atkins, John Webber, Jim Graham, Andrew Radford, Ronnie Clydesdale, Jim Kerr, Bruce Sangster and Ferrier Richardson. If you are a chef and would like more information on the Scottish Chefs Association, write to Brian Hannan, 16 St Brides Rd, Glasgow G43 2DU.

ENJOY A REAL
'FLAVOUR OF SCOTLAND'

All the recipes featured in this book have been produced by chefs. If you wish to visit their restaurants, here are the details:

David Wilson, Peat Inn, Fife KY15 5LH. Tel: 0133 484 0206

Hilary Brown, La Potiniere, Main St, Gullane, East Lothian EH31 2AA. Tel: 0162 084 3214

Ronnie Clydesdale, Ubiquitous Chip, 12 Ashton Lane, Glasgow G12 8SJ. Tel: 0141 334 5007

Frances Atkins, Shaws, 119 Old Brompton Rd, London SW7. Tel: 0171 373 4472

Nick Nairn, Braeval Old Mill, By Aberfoyle FK8 3UY. Tel: 0187 737 2711

Jim Graham, Ostlers Close, Bonnygate, Cupar, Fife KY15 4BU. Tel: 0133 465 5574

Keith and Nicola Braidwood, Braidwoods, Drumastle Mill Cottage, By Dalry, Ayrshire. Tel: 0129 483 3544

John Webber, Kinnaird, Kinnaird Estate, Near Dunkeld, Perthshire PH8 0LB. Tel: 0179 648 2440

Ferrier Richardson, Yes!, 22-24 West Nile St, Glasgow. Tel: 0141 221 8044

Betty Allen, Airds Hotel, Port Appin, Appin, Argyll PA38 4DF. Tel: 0163 173 236

Andrew Radford, The Atrium, 10 Cambridge St, Edinburgh EH1 2ED. Tel: 0131 228 8882

Bruce Sangster is executive chef for Lehman Brothers in the City of London. Unfortunately, unless invited, you cannot eat there.

NOTE ON MEASUREMENTS

In following a recipe, you should choose one set of measurements – imperial or metric – and stick with it. Recipes will not work if you move between metric and imperial within a single recipe.

Imperial	approx. metric equivalent
1oz	25g
2oz	50g
3oz	75g
4oz	100-125g
5oz	150g
6oz	175g
7oz	200g
8oz	225g
9oz	250g
10oz	275g
11oz	300g
12oz	350g
13oz	375g
14oz	400g
15oz	425g
16oz (1lb)	450g
1 fl oz	25ml
2 fl oz	50ml
5 fl oz (¼pt)	150ml
10 fl oz (½pt)	300ml
15 fl oz (¾pt)	450ml
35 fl oz	1 litre

Temperatures

deg C	deg F	Gas Mark
290	550	
270	525	
250	500	
240	475	9
230	450	8
220	425	7
200	400	6
190	375	5
180	350	4
170	325	3
150	300	2
140	275	1
130	250	½
110	225	¼
100	200	Low
80	175	
70	150	

CHAPTER ONE

DAVID WILSON

PIGEON has become something of a signature dish for the Peat Inn so one of the dishes I've chosen to do is *breast of pigeon on a confit of pork and butter-beans with a meat jus.* This dish also shows that the influences on modern Scottish cooking are worldwide.

Pigeon is an ideal dish to use because it's available all year round. Availability was certainly one reason I looked at it in the first place. For a restaurant, the late winter and early spring are the most difficult times for fresh produce – the game season is over, spring lamb has not started and fish supplies can be erratic because of the weather. But pigeon has no season, and I can rest assured on quality.

Even so, I put the dish on for the first time with some trepidation because pigeon had a terrible image problem in Scotland. It was perceived as tough and dry and gamey. But the reason for this was that it was overcooked and overhung. No hanging is necessary, and using a shorter cooking time achieved quite different results. The cooking time really is short – a few minutes as opposed to the old idea of cooking it for 35–40 minutes. As it transpired, my worries were groundless, for the dish, cooked in the new way, was an instant success.

When I first started using pigeon it was as a chartreuse. I presented a dish of chopped pigeon meat and vegetables wrapped in cabbage leaf. I've developed a number of different recipes using pigeon, and the one presented here has an Oriental influence. Pork is rarely used in restaurants, but it fits in quite well with the current mode of cooking with herbs and spices. Pork goes very well with pigeon because pork is fatty, whereas game, apart from duck, is not. The Chinese use a lot of pork in their cuisine, and it seemed logical in using pork to make it spicy. Of course, the butter beans aren't Oriental. The idea for using butter beans really came from the French dish cassoulet, which also has beans and pork. The butter beans complement the game and the meat very well.

There are a number of different influences in my *Scottish salmon with Szechuan peppercorns and celeriac purée*. The most important is a different approach to cooking salmon, and the dish relies, to some extent, on cooking something most people would usually throw away – the skin. Fish – like meat and game – should be undercooked. If you cook fish like salmon right through, it goes dry and white, and you lose the real flavour and succulence. For this dish I grill the fish. The big advantage of grilling over steaming or poaching is that you can cook the skin. In this dish, the skin is an important part of the flavour. Salmon skin is very, very tasty. The skin has natural oils, and when you cut into it there is a lovely flavour. But you can't eat it unless it's extremely crisp, so for this dish I cook it on one side. This results in the top side with the skin being burnt to a crisp crust while the underside is undercooked and succulent. When you cut through the salmon, it is still lovely and moist, with a good, bright colour. Fish is too delicate for ordinary peppercorns so I use Szechuan peppercorns, which are very mild and aromatic. I hadn't used these peppercorns before but I knew that I didn't want something that was going to be too hot on the tongue. The Szechuan variety is just right. The peppers are on the side that is cooked, so the aromatic flavour goes right into the flesh.

DAVID WILSON and his wife, Patricia, have completely transformed the Peat Inn near Cupar, in Fife, since they bought it in 1972. Then it was a typical Scottish pub in an untypical location, more or less in the middle of nowhere. At that time food was rarely served in Scottish pubs, and the menu David put on in the pub – pâté and quiche and crab salad – was unusual for the time. David was a self-taught chef, and there were times when he wondered why he had given up a secure job as a group marketing manager. But gradually, he improved his culinary skills, and the business began to grow, so much so that by 1979 they decided to run the place just as a restaurant. In 1987 David and Patricia took another major step by adding eight bedroom suites in a separate building within the garden which they call The Residence. Looking back over the past 23 years, what has given the couple the most pleasure is the wonderful people who supply the kind of produce they want. Many of them are virtually one-person businesses who, like the Wilsons, love what they are doing and are dedicated to giving the best or the unusual, whether it means growing, picking or shooting it. David Wilson was Scotland's first superstar chef, but the Wilsons' proudest moment was winning the industry's 'Oscar' – the Catey Award for Restaurateur of the Year in 1989, the first time the award had gone outside London. David is a founder member of the Scottish Chefs Association and sits on its Advisory Board.

Roast saddle of venison with lentils and smoked bacon

SERVES 4

This is a simple dish, with very little cooking time. The lentils and crispy bacon add a very good flavour and texture.

1lb (500g) piece saddle of venison, boned and trimmed
salt/pepper
oil for frying
12oz (350g) lentils plus 1 onion and a clove
4oz (100–125g) smoked bacon, cut into pieces approx. 10cm square
12 fl oz (500ml) game stock
1oz (25g) unsalted butter

1. Season venison with salt and pepper.
2. Put a little oil in a heavy sauté pan. When hot, place piece of venison in pan, turning to seal all sides. Continue to cook over a high heat for about 2 minutes, then transfer to a warm tray and place in centre of a preheated oven 400°F/200°C/Gas Mark, 6 cooking for a further 7 minutes, then put aside in warm place to rest for 20 minutes.
3. Wash and rinse lentils. Put in pan of cold water with an onion studded with a clove, and cook for about 45 minutes until tender.
4. Cook bacon in a preheated pan until crispy, just 3 or 4 minutes.
5. Reduce game stock until thick enough to coat the back of a spoon, then whisk in butter in small pieces. Season.

To serve the dish
Mix smoked-bacon pieces with lentils, spoon on to large warm serving dish. Place cooked venison on top. Add juices to sauce, spoon over venison.

Ragout of scallops, monkfish and pork with spiced apple

SERVES 4

Pork and apple are a popular combination, but when they become part of the scallop-and-monkfish ragout the result is an excellent flavour. The spices really lift the pork and apple.

8oz (225g) belly pork
chicken stock
vinaigrette sauce
4oz (100–125g) monkfish fillet
8 scallops
1 Granny Smith apple
1 level tsp mixed spices, including coriander, cumin, cinnamon, nutmeg,
    allspice, caraway, ginger, cloves and cardamon

1. Dice belly pork into pieces about $^1/_2$in. ($1^1/_4$cm) square, then pre-cook in a little chicken stock until very tender (about 45 minutes).
2. Make vinaigrette sauce (see recipe below).
3. Slice monkfish fillet into thin slices and the scallops in half. Reserve roes of scallops.
4. Strain pork, then place on flat tray and grill under preheated grill until crisp.
5. Peel and core apple. Using size 10 or 12 parisienne scoop, make apple balls (if no scoop, dice into $^1/_4$in./6mm dice).
6. Add apple balls to pork, sprinkle the spices over pork and apple, then reheat under grill.
7. Put some sunflower oil in sauté pan, heat until it begins to smoke. Fry monkfish slices for about 2 minutes each side. Keep hot, then in same pan, fry scallops and roes about one minute each side.

Vinaigrette sauce
1 fl oz (50ml) virgin olive oil
$^1/_2$ fl oz (25ml) red-wine vinegar
1 tsp soy sauce
$^1/_2$ fl oz (25ml) walnut oil
salt/pepper
sunflower oil for frying

To serve the dish
Spoon pork and apple on to centre of warm plate, place scallops and monkfish on top. Spoon warm vinaigrette on top and around.

Breast of pigeon on a confit of pork and butter-beans with a meat jus

SERVES 4

Two of the most underrated items of produce combine in a dish that's easy to make and can be used in different ways.

2lb (1kg) trimmed pork shoulder
1 level dessertspoon Chinese spices
1 level tsp sea-salt
$^1/_2$ cup soy sauce
1 tsp lemon juice
4oz (100–125g) butter-beans
vegetable oil for frying
1pt (600ml) chicken stock
2 tomatoes, skin off and de-seeded
4 pigeon breasts
$^1/_2$pt (300ml) good brown beef stock
1oz (25g) unsalted butter

1. 24 hours in advance dice pork into approx. $^1/_2$in. pieces. Place in glass or non-reactive bowl. Sprinkle over spice, sea-salt, soy sauce and lemon juice. Cover with cling film and refrigerate.
2. 8 hours in advance or overnight, put butter-beans in bowl or pan. Cover with cold water and leave to soak, changing the water 2 or 3 times.
3. At the time of cooking, remove pork from bowl, reserving marinade liquid. Seal pork off in sauté pan preheated using a little vegetable oil. Transfer to casserole or saucepan, add chicken stock, cover and simmer for about 2 hours or until tender.
4. Drain butter-beans then place in pan of salted water. Bring to boil. Boil for 5 minutes. Drain, then add to pork. Simmer for 20 minutes, adding tomato chopped into large pieces for last 5 minutes.
5. To cook pigeon breasts put a film of vegetable oil in a sauté pan. When hot, place pigeon breasts skin-side down in pan. Cook on skin side for about 3 minutes, then transfer to warm tray and place in preheated oven 400°F/200°C/Gas Mark 6 for a further 3 minutes. Remove and transfer to cool oven or warm place to rest.

6. To make jus, add marinade juices to beef stock. Reduce by about one third then whisk in butter in small pieces. Check seasoning – remember there was salt in marinade so it may not need adjusting.

To serve the dish
Spoon pork and beans on to centre of warm plate. Cut pigeon breast diagonally in three but not right through. Place breast on top of pork, then pour sauce over and around.

Roast young grouse

SERVES 4

Grouse is very easy to cook and takes hardly any time at all. Because the basic produce is so good, fresh young grouse requires only minimal preparation.

4 young grouse
salt/pepper
2oz (50g) butter
4 rashers bacon
sauce (see recipe below)

1. If you have not had your supplier prepare the birds, you must carefully pluck and draw them, reserving the liver if you wish to use it (optional). To avoid feathers all over your kitchen, it may be more sensible to carry out this task working with the birds inside a large cardboard box in your garage or outhouse. Chop off the feet at the joints.
2. Preheat your oven to 400°F/200°C/Gas Mark 6.
3. Season birds inside and out with salt and pepper, putting a knob of butter inside the cavity.
4. Put a piece of bacon over the breast, place birds on roasting tray and put tray on centre shelf of oven.
5. Roast for 10–12 minutes only – test for readiness by pressing the breast between finger and thumb: there should be some resilience.
6. Remove from oven and leave to rest for 5 minutes in a warm place.
7. Remove legs, then breasts. Keep legs and breasts on a tray in a warm place. Chop 2 of the carcases for sauce (see recipe below).

Sauce

Approx. $^1/_2$pt game stock or brown chicken stock
Bones from carcase of grouse, chopped
1oz (25g) unsalted butter
salt/pepper

1. Put stock with chopped carcases in saucepan, bring to boil then simmer for 5 minutes.
2. Strain through fine sieve into other saucepan, pressing bones with back of ladle to extract all the juices.
3. Bring this sauce back to simmer, reduce approximately by half, then finish sauce by whisking in diced butter over a low heat. Check sauce, season to taste.

To serve the dish

Remove skin from legs and breasts. Arrange legs and breasts attractively on warm plates. Pour sauce around, garnish with some game chips and serve a well-dressed green salad on the side. Optional: the livers can be lightly sautéd in clarified butter and spread on a fried crouton, then placed on the plate above the breasts. The best accompaniment is some sauté potatoes and a green salad.

Whole lobster in a vegetable-and-herb broth

SERVES 4

This is a very different and unusual method of cooking lobster, with the aromatic broth enhancing the natural flavour of the lobster.

1/4 cup olive oil
1 tbsp chopped shallots
1 clove garlic, crushed
1 tsp tomato purée
2 cups vegetable stock
1 level tsp fresh thyme
1 bay leaf, pulverised
2oz (50g) unsalted butter, diced
2 tbsp crème fraîche
4 lobsters
1 tbsp carrot, finely sliced (precooked and refreshed)
1 tbsp fennel, finely sliced (precooked and refreshed)
1 tbsp leek, finely sliced (precooked and refreshed)
1 tbsp fresh tarragon, finely chopped
1 tbsp fresh basil, finely chopped
1 tbsp fresh chives, snipped

1. To prepare broth, put olive oil in saucepan over a low heat. Add shallots and garlic. Cook until soft but without colouring.
2. Add tomato purée and vegetable stock, then stir in thyme and bay leaf.
3. Whisk in butter, then add crème fraîche. Check seasoning at time of serving.
4. To cook the lobsters, bring a large pan to boil. Place lobsters in boiling water and return to boil and cook for 10 minutes.
5. Remove from pan, allow to cool slightly, then remove claws.
6. Remove meat from claws. Put tail side down on chopping-board. Press firmly with palm of hand to crack, then, turning tail on its back, pull shell off using your thumbs on each side to pull apart. Cut tail meat through at each joint.

To serve the dish

Place lobster tail in centre of warm plate and claws at each side to create the shape of the lobster. Scatter the finely sliced carrot, fennel and leek around, pour over broth, then sprinkle with fresh herbs. Serve immediately.

28

Scottish salmon with Szechuan peppercorns

SERVES 4

This dish is so easy to make and provides a lovely aromatic flavour for the salmon.

1lb (450g) celeriac
$^1/_2$pt (300ml) vegetable stock
$^1/_4$pt (150ml) double cream
1oz (25g) unsalted butter, diced
seasoning
$^1/_4$pt (150ml) good-quality brown stock
1tsp dark soy sauce
1oz (25g) unsalted butter, diced
4 (100–125g) salmon fillets, about 4oz each, skin left on, descaled and bones
    removed
sea-salt
2 tbsp Szechuan peppercorns
vegetable oil

1. To make the purée, peel and dice the celeriac, then cook it in a pan of boiling salted water until soft. Drain, then purée in a food processor until smooth. Return to the pan. Add the vegetable stock and double cream. Reheat gently, stirring continuously. Whisk in the butter. Season and set aside.
2. To make the spiced brown sauce, bring the brown stock to the boil and add the soy sauce. Simmer uncovered, until the liquid is reduced and thick enough to coat the back of a spoon. Whisk in the butter. Season and set aside.
3. To prepare the salmon, slash the skin 5 or 6 times with a sharp knife. Sprinkle over some sea-salt, then cover fairly generously with the peppercorns, pressing them on to the skin.
4. Heat a little vegetable oil in a sauté pan until it begins to smoke, then place the salmon, skin-side down, in the pan and cook for 3 minutes. Remove from the pan, transfer to a baking sheet, skin-side up, and cook under a moderate grill for 3–5 minutes, until skin is crisp but the flesh moist.

To serve the dish
Spoon the celeriac purée on to warmed plates. Drizzle brown sauce around the edge of the purée, then top with a salmon fillet. Serve immediately.

Millefeuille of hazelnut meringue and red fruits with an orange sabayon sauce

SERVES 4

This is an interesting and dramatic way of creating an attractive dish that shows off the full flavour of the lovely fresh fruits available in Scotland in late summer.

meringue (see recipe below)
vanilla cream (see recipe below)
4oz (100–125g) strawberries
4oz (100–125g) raspberries
icing sugar
redcurrants (optional)
mint leaves
orange sabayon sauce (see recipe below)

Meringues
10 egg whites
10oz (275g) caster sugar
7oz (200g) finely ground hazelnuts

1. Beat egg whites until stiff, along with half the amount of sugar.
2. Sift remaining sugar and hazelnuts together and fold delicately into whipped egg whites.
3. Pipe on to greased baking sheet to make approx. 12 3-in. rounds.
4. Cook in oven at 250°F/125°C/Gas Mark 1 until meringues are crisp and slightly golden in colour.

Vanilla cream
3oz (100g) caster sugar
1pt (600ml) milk
6 egg yolks
1 heaped tbsp plain flour
1 rounded dessertspoon cornflour
$1/2$ vanilla pod, split
1pt (600ml) double cream

1. Bring half of sugar to boil in pint of milk, stirring until sugar dissolves.
2. Whip 6 egg yolks with remaining sugar until light and fluffy.
3. Sieve the two flours into the yolk mixture and fold it in.
4. Add half of the boiled milk/sugar, whisk for a minute, then add to remainder of milk. Add vanilla pod.
5. Bring to simmering point and simmer for about 2 minutes, then allow to cool. Whip the double cream and fold together.

Orange sabayon sauce
3oz (100g) caster sugar
4 egg yolks
$1/2$pt (300ml) dry white wine
squeeze lemon juice
dash Grand Marnier (optional)

1. Mix the ingredients together.
2. Whisk in a bain-marie over a gentle heat until mixture thickens – do not boil.

To serve the dish
Place meringue on centre of plate. Spread some vanilla cream on top, then a layer of strawberries. Place second meringue on top of strawberries (carefully) and more vanilla cream on top, and then place some raspberries on. Place third meringue on top. Sprinkle with icing sugar and decorate with a red fruit and fresh mint leaf. Pour sabayon sauce around.

Trio of caramel desserts with a caramel sauce

SERVES 4

This dessert, as the title implies, is in three parts, with each part having several secondary parts plus the sauce. The dish consists of caramel ice-cream in an almond tuille biscuit cup, caramelised apple pastry and crème caramels. There is also a caramel sauce, so there are five recipes in all.

Almond tuille biscuit cup
4 egg whites
1 whole egg
7oz (200g) caster sugar
3oz (90g) sieved plain flour
1 heaped tsp flaked almonds
1 tsp almond essence
$3^{1}/_{2}$ dessertspoons melted butter

1. Whip egg whites until stiff.
2. Add whole egg, then fold in caster sugar, flour, flaked almonds and almond essence. Finally, add melted butter.
3. Using a buttered baking tray drop one dessertspoon of the mixture on to tray. Repeat to create 4 separate biscuits. Place in centre of preheated oven and bake at 325°F/170°C/Gas Mark 3 until golden.
4. Remove from oven, and while still hot remove biscuits from tray and place over small bowl to form shape. When cool, store in an airtight container until required. Repeat with remainder of mixture.

Caramel ice-cream
$4^{1}/_{2}$oz (125g) granulated sugar
$^{1}/_{2}$ vanilla pod, split
scant $^{1}/_{4}$pt (150ml) double cream
6 egg yolks
$^{1}/_{4}$pt (150ml) milk

1. Make caramel by dissolving sugar and vanilla pod in heavy-based saucepan until sugar becomes deep golden brown in colour.
2. Remove from heat, then stir in cream.
3. Beat egg yolks until they are a thick consistency and cream colour.

4. Bring milk to boil. Add to egg yolks. Mix thoroughly.
5. Put caramel mixture into double boiler, then pour egg/milk mixture into caramel mixture. Heat in double boiler until mixture thickens.
6. Allow to cool, then place in ice-cream machine.

Caramelised apple pastry
2oz (50g) granulated sugar
water
3 Granny Smith apples
approx. 4oz (100–125g) puff pastry (leftover scraps will do)
icing sugar
4 apple balls (size-10 parisienne scoop)
4 sprigs sweet cicily to garnish (optional)
$^1/_2$ vanilla pod, split

1. To make caramel syrup to cook apples, heat sugar until it begins to caramelise to deep golden colour. Add $^1/_2$pt (300ml) water and vanilla.
2. Peel and core apples. Dice into squares approx. $^3/_8$in. (10mm).
3. Put diced apple in syrup. Bring back to boil, then take off heat. Leave to cool.
4. Roll pastry out as thin as possible no more than $^1/_{16}$in. (3mm) thick. Lift pastry on rolling-pin and place on baking sheet. Place second baking sheet on top weighted down by 2x2lb (1kg) kitchen weights or a heavy object (this stops the puff pastry from rising). Place in centre of preheated oven at 450°F/225°C/Gas Mark 8 and cook for about 12 minutes until pastry is golden brown.

To assemble
Cut pastry into 2in. (50mm) squares. Dust 4 squares with icing sugar, then make scores on top with a hot skewer. Place other squares on plates, spoon cooked apple on top, then place scored pastry on top. Garnish with leaf or sweet cicily and apple ball.

Crème caramels
1pt (600ml) double cream
$^1/_2$ vanilla pod, split
$3^1/_2$oz (100g) caster sugar
2 whole eggs
4 egg yolks
2oz (50g) caster sugar
$2^1/_2$ fl oz (approx. $^1/_4$pt) boiling water

1. Bring cream to boil with vanilla pod.
2. Combine sugar and eggs in pan. Pour sugar-and-egg mixture into cream and mix thoroughly.
3. Make a caramel syrup by placing caster sugar in pan and heat until sugar turns dark, golden brown, then add boiling water.
4. Run caramel around inside of small pots approx. 2in. (50mm) deep x $1^3/_4$in. (45mm). Pour egg-custard mixture into pots, then place pots in tray with hot water approx. halfway up sides of pots. Cover loosely with aluminium foil, then place in centre of preheated oven. Cook at 250°F/130°C/Gas Mark $^1/_2$ for about 2 hours or until set.

Caramel sauce
1x14oz (400g) tin condensed milk
3oz (100g) unsalted butter
8oz (225g) granulated sugar
3 dessertspoons syrup
1 dessertspoon liquid glucose
$^1/_2$ vanilla pod, split
1pt (600ml) boiling water

1. Empty contents of tin of condensed milk into saucepan. Add all other ingredients *except water.*
2. Place saucepan on heat, bring to boil, lower heat and allow to simmer gently, stirring continuously for 20 minutes.
3. Remove from heat, add boiled water carefully as it will 'spit' when it first makes contact with caramel. Sieve, then leave to cool until required.

To serve the dish
Run the warm caramel sauce around plate. In the top-left corner place almond tuille biscuit, then fill this with a scoop of caramel ice-cream. Put square of pastry at top-right corner, then spoon some caramelised apples on top. Place scored square on top and garnish with apple ball and sweet cicily (optional). Turn out crème caramel on to bottom centre of plate (you may have to run a sharp knife around this to loosen it from pot). Serve immediately.

CHAPTER TWO

HILARY BROWN

I HADN'T cooked very much salmon until in a restaurant in France I ate some which had been cooked in the frying-pan. Up until then salmon was something I had assumed was either grilled as a steak or poached as a whole fish. I suddenly realised that salmon offered a lot more potential.

My *salmon on spicy lentils* is cooked in hazelnut oil very quickly and is moist and lightly cooked inside. I started doing lentil bases with wild mushrooms for a chicken-breast dish. With the chicken dish it didn't have the spices, but for the salmon that seemed to work well. The gutsy, coarse texture of the salmon works with the gutsy lentils.

I tend to have a picture of a dish in my head from the start and work towards achieving that, thinking about flavour and technique along the way. If something works, I don't change it for the sake of change. If I wanted to do something else, I'd rather do something completely different.

Cooking the salmon gave me the confidence to try other types of fish. In the past my fish cooking had tended towards mousselines rather than taking a bit of fish and cooking it simply. Once I was more confident, I started cooking sole very, very quickly in a hot oven. When we first bought this restaurant 20 years ago, we had an old cooker that couldn't heat very high. With our new oven, we can cook something at 500°F for five minutes, which would have been impossible in the past. *Sole with pesto, virgin olive-oil sauce and crispy courgettes* is an updated version of the recipe which appeared in our recipe book, *La Potiniere and Friends.*

While I don't really have a favourite course, if I've got nothing to do in the afternoon and want to experiment, it's puddings I'd rather make. When I was at college, I used to come home and cook for the sake of cooking, and it was always puddings and cakes. My enjoyment of puddings dates back to then. I made puddings because I find them satisfying, not because I want to eat them. I don't really eat puddings at all.

HILARY BROWN set up La Potiniere with her husband, David, 20 years ago. She has a Michelin star. A book of recipes by Hilary Brown, entitled *La Potiniere and Friends*, can be obtained only from the restaurant. Hilary is a founder member of the Scottish Chefs Association and sits on its Advisory Board.

Potage St Germain

SERVES 6

This is one of my favourite dishes. Careful cooking is necessary for its striking colour and delicious flavour. Obviously, it's important to use the right peas, and I use Bird's Eye Country Club.

8oz (225g) onions
4oz (100–125g) lettuce
2oz (50g) unsalted butter
1lb (450g) frozen peas
1 heaped tsp dried mint or 2 heaped tsp chopped fresh mint
seasoning
2oz (50g) petits pois
little lightly whipped cream to garnish
sprig of fresh mint to garnish

1. Peel and slice the onions. Trim and chop the lettuce.
2. Melt the butter in a medium-sized saucepan and add the sliced onion. Cook gently until the onion is softened but not brown.
3. Add the lettuce leaves and stir together with a wooden spoon. Add $^1/_2$pt (300ml) water and simmer for about 40 minutes.
4. Liquidise until smooth. Pour through a mouli into a bowl.
5. Place the peas in the same pan, cover with $^1/_2$pt (300ml) water and bring to the boil as quickly as possible. As soon as the water comes to the boil, remove from the heat, pour into the liquidiser, add the mint, and blend until smooth. Pour through the mouli into the bowl containing the onion-and-lettuce mixture.
6. Stir together, season to taste, add water if necessary, and return to the rinsed-out pan. The mixture should not be too thin or it will lose its character.
7. When ready to serve the soup, reheat it over a medium heat. Add the petits pois. Do not allow the soup to boil for more than a minute or two as the colour is easily impaired.

To serve the dish
Serve in warmed bowls or a tureen. Garnish with a little whipped cream and fresh mint.

Tomato-and-basil soup

SERVES 6

Use tomatoes that are as ripe and as red as possible (without being blemished in any way). Plum tomatoes have a particularly good flavour. Ring the changes by using mint instead of basil.

8oz (225g) onions
2oz (50g) unsalted butter
2lb (900g) tomatoes, the redder the better
3 fl oz (75ml) dry sherry
1 tbsp caster sugar
1 pack fresh basil $^3/_4$oz (20g)
seasoning
sprigs of fresh basil for garnish
a little lightly whipped cream for garnish

1. Peel and finely slice the onions. Melt the butter in a medium-sized saucepan. Add the onion and cook gently until softened but not coloured. Stir from time to time with a wooden spoon.
2. Add the tomatoes whole, with skins and stalks, the sherry and sugar. No water is required at this stage. Stir together, cover with a lid, then simmer for 45 minutes to an hour. Stir occasionally.
3. Ladle the mixture into a liquidiser and blend until smooth. Drop the fresh basil into the liquidiser and continue to blend for 15 seconds.
4. Pour the soup through a mould into the rinsed-out pan.
5. Stir together, then add enough water to correct the consistency. Season to taste, about 1–2 tsp salt. It should have plenty of body so do not add too much water. The tomatoes should have created enough liquid.
6. Reheat the soup when wishing to serve.

To serve the dish
Ladle into warmed soup bowls or one large tureen. Garnish with a little lightly whipped cream, topped with a sprig of fresh basil.

Salmon on spicy lentils

SERVES 6

This is a fairly heavy dish, with an unusual combination of spices, lentils, wild mushroom and salmon. It can be served as a starter or main course.

3oz (75g) white part of leek
1 clove garlic
2lb (900g) middle-cut salmon
1^1/$_2$oz (40g) unsalted butter
1 heaped tsp spices – grind equal quantities of cumin, fennel, coriander, and
    cardamon seeds together. I use an electric coffee-grinder.
6oz (175g) lentil du Puy
10 fl oz (300ml) home-made stock
5 fl oz (150ml) Noilly Prat
5 fl oz (150ml) double cream
6 large dried morilles, or 12 to 18 small ones
Maldon sea-salt
1 tbs hazelnut oil

1. Finely dice the leek and peel and crush the garlic, bone the salmon into two fillets. Run your fingers over the fish to check for bones and remove with tweezers. Cut each side into three, then cut each of these crosswise, giving 6 squarish pieces, removing the skin as you do so. Set aside covered with cling film until needed.
2. Melt ^{1}/$_2$oz (15g) butter in a small pan. Add the diced leek and crushed garlic and spices. Cook, stirring frequently until softened.
3. Meanwhile, rinse the lentils, place in a pan, cover with cold water, and bring to the boil. Boil for two minutes, then strain. Return to the pan, add 5 fl oz (150ml) stock, the leek mixture and ^{1}/$_2$oz (15g) butter. Set aside until needed.
4. For the sauce, place Noilly Prat in a pan, bring to the boil, and reduce by two-thirds. Add the remaining 5 fl oz (150ml) stock and reduce by half, add the cream and the final ^{1}/$_2$oz (15g) butter and simmer until a thin sauce consistency is reached.
5. While the sauce is reducing, place the morilles in a bowl and pour boiling water over. Allow to soak for 10 minutes, then squeeze dry and add to the sauce.
6. When ready to serve, reheat the lentils and cook until they become softened

without reaching a mush stage. Season with a little salt. Gently reheat the sauce and taste for seasoning.

7. Place a heavy frying-pan on a high heat and let it become very hot. Add 1 tbsp hazelnut oil, swirl it around, then place the salmon (ex-skin-side up) in the pan. Cook for 1 minute, turn over using tongs and, after another minute, turn over again. The salmon will be cooked after 4–5 minutes, depending on the thickness. It should be crisp and brown on the outside, moist and lightly cooked inside.

To serve the dish

Place a tbsp of the lentil mixture on to 6 heated serving plates. Spoon a tbsp of sauce around. Set the salmon at an angle on top and sprinkle with crushed Maldon sea-salt. Serve immediately.

Boned guinea-fowl legs with apricot-and-mint stuffing

SERVES 6

I always use a lot of breast of guinea-fowl and was wondering what to do with leg when I came up with an idea of Nico Ladenis's. In his book, he has a recipe using brioche with herbs to stuff a fillet of veal. I've adapted the idea for stuffing guinea-fowl leg. For the stuffing, I experimented with dried apricots and mint and thought that combination worked well.

2^1/$_2$oz (65g) unsulphured dried apricots
1tsp black peppercorns
^{1}/$_4$oz (7g) fresh mint leaves
1 egg (size 2)
^{1}/$_4$ tsp salt
4oz (100–125g) brioche breadcrumbs
6 boned guinea-fowl legs
6 dessertspoons runny honey
2 dessertspoons apricot and apple concentrate (available from health-food shops)
1^1/$_2$oz (40g) unsalted butter
4 tbsp double cream

1. Cut the dried apricots into ^{1}/$_4$in. (^{3}/$_4$cm) squares. Coarsely crush the peppercorns.
2. Place the mint leaves in the bowl of your food processor, fitted with the cutting blade (if the breadcrumbs were made in the processor, there is no need to wash it out). Blend until chopped. Then add the egg (break it in a ramekin as you don't want to risk any of the shell falling in). Continue to blend, adding the salt.
3. Combine the breadcrumbs, mint mixture and apricot cubes in a bowl. Mix together well.
4. Lay the opened, boned legs on your chopping-board, and, using a spatula or flat-bladed knife, stuff them with the mixture. Press gently down into the 'calf' end. Bring the two edges together to form a sausage shape.
5. Using a sterilised needle and ordinary thread, sew the edges together. Leave one end about 2in. (5cm) long, so that it makes removing it easier. Gently roll each leg like a piece of plasticine to form it into an even shape.

6. At this stage, the legs can be covered and refrigerated until required – they can be made the day before, but no earlier. Remove the legs from the fridge at least an hour before you wish to start cooking them.

7. Preheat the oven to 375°F/190°C/Gas Mark 5. Butter an ovenproof tray and lay the legs on it, not touching each other. Mix the honey and pepper together and spoon over each leg.

8. Bake in the preheated oven, on the middle shelf, for 30 minutes – less if using a fan oven.

9. Meanwhile, place the stock and concentrated juice in a medium-sized pan. Bring to the boil and reduce by half. Add the butter and cream and continue to reduce, whisking occasionally, until a slightly syrupy sauce is formed. Taste for seasoning, but it is unlikely that you will need any.

10. When the legs are cooked, remove from the oven. Remove the thread – a pair of rubber gloves and a pointed knife are useful at this stage. Pull the thread from one end in one piece.

11. Slice into five or six pieces.

To serve the dish

Using a serrated knife, arrange the meat in overlapping circles on warmed serving plates. Spoon over a couple of tbsp of sauce.

Breast of game bird on a purée of Brussels sprouts with spicy red-wine sauce and cranberries

SERVES 6

This is a very seasonal dish, using ingredients which are associated with Christmas. Pheasant, mallard and guinea-fowl are particularly successful.

The breasts of 3 birds – either hen pheasants (more tender than cocks), mallard or guinea-fowl
1 dessertspoon hazelnut oil
1 dessertspoon olive oil
$1^1/_2$ tsp Chinese five spice
10 fl oz (just under 300ml) red wine
2 level tsp redcurrant jelly
10 fl oz (just under 300ml) home-made stock (make the day before, using the carcases of the birds)
1lb (450g) prepared Brussels sprouts – large supermarkets sell bags of pre-prepared ones
$2^1/_2$oz (65g) unsalted butter
3 tbsp whipping cream
2oz (50g) cranberries

1. Preferably the day before, if using whole birds, remove the breast of each one. Remove the skin and place the breasts in a bowl. Spoon the oils over them and sprinkle with 1 tsp of the spices. Mix well (a rubber-gloved hand is good for this), then cover with cling film. Refrigerate overnight.
2. Preheat your oven to 475°F/240°C/Gas Mark 9. Remove the breasts from the refrigerator at least an hour before cooking them.
3. Place the red wine, jelly and $^1/_2$ tsp spice in a pan. Bring to the boil and reduce until only about 3 tbsp remain. (Don't do what I have often done – forgotten all about it and wondered what the awful burning smell and cloud of smoke is all about!) Add the stock and continue to reduce. Add 2oz (50g) butter, and once it reaches a light-sauce consistency, turn off.
4. Meanwhile, place the sprouts in a pan large enough to take them in a layer or two. Add 5 fl oz (150ml) cold water. Cover with a lid and bring to the boil. Cook for about 5 minutes. For appearance, nutritional and taste's sake, don't overcook. Test with a pointed knife. They should pierce easily without being soft or discoloured. Drain off any remaining water. Add $^1/_2$oz (15g) butter

and the cream. Using a Braun hand 'wand', blend the sprouts to a fairly fine purée.

5. Place a frying-pan over a high heat and allow it to become very hot. When hot, place the breasts in the pan, leaving a little space between each one. (If your frying-pan is small, don't squeeze them in – do this stage in two batches.) Sprinkle with a little salt, then turn over. Cook for another few seconds, then place on an ovenproof tray. This stage is just to brown the breasts, not to cook them. If you are not ready to cook them, they can sit on the tray for an hour or so.

6. Place in the oven and bake for 9 minutes. Meanwhile, check the sauce. Whisk it over a medium heat (if it has separated a little, add 1 tbsp cold water) and, once hot, add the cranberries. Cook *very* gently, as your aim is to heat the cranberries, not to burst them. Gently reheat the sprout purée, stirring with a wooden spoon – be careful, as it tends to stick.

French dressing

A dressing can make or mar a salad. A good one, using interesting oil and good vinegar, can transform simple salad leaves into something very delicious. There are so many different oils to choose from, and which one you use depends on your taste and their availability. Nut oils, such as hazelnut and walnut, have a very strong but lovely flavour, and, if added to olive oil, make a French dressing more interesting. If using a nut oil as well as olive oil, it would be a waste to use virgin olive oil as the flavours would compete.

MAKES $1^1/_4$PT (750ML)
15 fl oz (450ml) olive oil
5 fl oz (150ml) walnut oil (refrigerate any left over)
$2^1/_2$ fl oz (65ml) sherry vinegar and $2^1/_2$ fl oz (65ml) white-wine vinegar
2 tsp salt
2 rounded tsp honey
2 tsp Moutarde de Meaux

1. Place all the ingredients in a liquidiser and blend for 30 seconds. Pour into a large, screwtop jar.
2. Shake well before using.
3. Refrigerate any left over.

To serve the dish

Place a spoonful of purée on each warm serving plate. Place the breasts on a chopping-board and, using a sharp knife, cut each into about 5 slices across, then place on the purée. Spoon a tbsp or so of the sauce over the breast and serve straight away.

NOTE

Rounds of gratin dauphinois (recipe in *La Potiniere and Friends*) heated along with the breasts (put them in a little earlier) go very well with this. Decorate with salad burnett leaves if you can get them.

Sole with pesto, virgin-olive-oil sauce and crispy courgettes

SERVES 6

Attractive to look at, with interesting flavours and textures, this dish can be prepared ahead, leaving only the cooking of the sole and spinach to the last minute.

6 fillets of lemon sole (approx. 3^1/$_2$oz/90g each)
pesto sauce (see recipe below)
virgin olive-oil sauce (see recipe below)
1^1/$_2$lb (675g) medium-sized, dark green courgettes
vegetable oil for deep frying – I use sunflower
12oz (350g) fresh spinach – washed and dried
1 packet fresh basil
^{1}/$_2$oz (15g) unsalted butter
seasoning

1. If necessary, skin the sole. If it has been already, by your fishmonger, it may well have a membrane left on it, which would cause the fish to curl up during cooking. If so, using a very sharp, pointed knife, cut a couple of slashes along this, without actually going right through the fish. Cover and refrigerate until needed.
2. Make pesto and transfer to a jamjar.
3. Make virgin-olive-oil sauce, with tomato or red pepper, depending on which suits the rest of the menu best.
4. Wash and dry the courgettes. Remove the ends. Preferably using a mandoline, cut into long matchsticks ^{1}/$_{16}$ in. x ^{1}/$_{16}$ in. (2mm x 2mm) x length of the courgette. Using your fingertips, lift and separate the strips from each other.
5. Heat the vegetable oil in a heavy pan. There should be about 1in. (3cm) oil. Once it reaches 375°F/190°C/Gas Mark 5 drop the strips into it (wearing rubber gloves will prevent you from being spattered with hot oil). Stir around, then leave to fry until they become golden brown. Have an ovenproof tray lined with a double layer of kitchen roll to hand, and, using a slotted spoon, transfer the crispy strips into it. 'Tease' them so that they are light and airy. Sprinkle with a tiny amount of salt.
6. If you have a juice extractor, press 3^1/$_2$oz (100g) of the spinach along with the basil into it and place a jamjar under the hole. Switch on. A small amount of

highly concentrated spinach and basil juice will pour into the jamjar. Cover and refrigerate until needed.

7. You now have all the components of the dish. To assemble it, preheat the oven to 475°F/240°C/Gas Mark 9. Lightly butter an ovenproof tray.

8. Lay the sole out on a chopping-board, ex-skin-side up. Season with a very little salt, then spread with a tsp of pesto. Fold over, with the thicker end placed over the tail end. Arrange the sole on the tray, leaving a little space between each one. Sprinkle with cold water and season lightly.

9. Place the remaining spinach in a large pan. Sprinkle with a little salt and add the remaining butter. Add a tsp of cold water and cover with a lid.

10. Place on a high heat, at the same time as sliding the sole into the preheated oven. The sole will take 5–6 minutes, depending on the thickness of the fish. Don't overcook it!

11. As soon as the spinach has 'wilted' drain through a colander or sieve. Shake to remove excess liquid.

Pesto sauce

1 medium garlic clove
$1^1/_2$oz (40g) Parmesan cheese
2oz (50g) fresh basil leaves
$1^1/_2$oz (40g) pine kernels
$^1/_4$tsp salt
3 fl oz (75ml) good olive oil

1. Peel the garlic and freshly grate the Parmesan.

2. Place all the ingredients except the oil in your food processor fitted with the cutting blade. Process until a purée is formed.

3. Continue to blend while adding the oil in a thin stream.

4. Stop the processor, lift off the lid and scrape down the mixture from the sides of the bowl.

5. Blend again so that all the ingredients are evenly mixed.

6. Scrape out into a jamjar and cover until required. It will keep for several weeks if refrigerated. The colour may change a little but it will still taste sensational. A little goes a long way and can also be used to liven up pasta, risotto and vegetables, etc.

Virgin-olive-oil sauce

2 fl oz (50ml) virgin olive oil
4 large fresh basil
a pinch of salt
1 small garlic clove with skin left on
1 large firm beef tomato or 2 smaller ones or $^1/_2$ firm red pepper

1. First of all choose an interesting olive oil. The only real way is tasting and trying different oils. Two that I use at the moment are *Badia a Coltibuono* and *Selvapiana*, both from Tuscany.
2. Finely chop the fresh basil.
3. Warm the olive oil in a small pan over a low heat.
4. Remove from the heat and add the basil, salt and the whole unpeeled clove of garlic. Let these flavours develop by leaving the pan aside for at least 1 hour.
5. Meanwhile, prepare the tomato(es). Cut down from the stalk end, then cut each half in two or three, depending on size. Cut out the seeds and core. Then place the pieces skin-side down. Flatten with one hand while cutting the flesh away from the skin with a small, sharp knife. Cut each piece into strips $^1/_4$in.(96mm) wide, then cut across diagonally to form diamond shapes (or cut into $^1/_4$in./6mm squares).
6. Alternatively, carefully slice the piece of red pepper in two, lengthwise, to give two thinner slices. Cut these into small dice, $^1/_8$in. (3mm) squares.
7. Add these to the oil shortly before serving. Place the small pan in a larger, shallower one containing a little simmering water. Heat together for about 10 minutes. Remove the garlic and serve a tbsp of sauce with the dish.

To serve the dish

Place equal quantities of spinach on 6 heated serving plates. Using a pointed spoon, dribble some virgin-olive-oil around it, then, using a teaspoon, make little blobs of the spinach and basil juice through the oil. Top with a piece of sole – use a fish slice to transfer it, then balance a mound of courgette strips on top. (Preheat them in the oven when you remove the sole – a minute is long enough.) Serve immediately.

David Wilson

WHOLE LOBSTER IN A VEGETABLE-AND-HERB BROTH

Hilary Brown
SOLE WITH PESTO, VIRGIN-OLIVE-OIL SAUCE AND CRISPY COURGETTES

Ronnie Clydesdale

SCOTCH MUTTON STUFFED WITH MUSSELS WITH A WHITE-WINE-AND-SHELLFISH SAUCE

HILARY BROWN

RONNIE CLYDESDALE

Lemon surprise pudding

SERVES 6

The surprise aspect of this is the separation which takes place during the cooking to form a light, spongy layer on a soft, curd-like base. We use ramekins which are decorated on the outside with twisting strips of lemon peel. To add to the 'surprise', once the pudding has been eaten, two cheeky lemon pips are found painted on the base.

2oz (50g) unsalted butter
2 eggs (size 2)
3$^{1}/_{2}$oz (90g) caster sugar
$^{1}/_{2}$oz (15g) plain flour
finely grated rind and juice of 1 lemon
8 fl oz (225ml) milk

1. Soften the butter and separate the eggs.
2. Place butter, egg yolks, sugar, flour and lemon rind in the food processor fitted with the cutting blade. Blend until smooth, adding the lemon juice, then the milk.
3. Pour the mixture into a bowl and leave for 1 hour.
4. Preheat oven to 350°F/180°C/Gas Mark 4. Place 6 ramekins – with a capacity of 5 fl oz (150ml) – in a bain marie, i.e. a container such as a roasting tin or pyrex dish which will take enough water to come halfway up the sides of the ramekins.
5. Place the egg whites in a spotless bowl. Using an electric hand-held beater or balloon whisk, beat until stiff. Fold into the lemon mixture gently but thoroughly with a large metal spoon.
6. Ladle into the ramekins, place on the front of the middle shelf of the oven, pour enough boiling water into the tin, then slide it in.
7. Bake undisturbed for 35–40 minutes, by which time they will be slightly risen, rounded on top and golden brown.

To serve the dish
Sprinkle the individual puddings with extra caster sugar, place on plates or saucers and serve straight away.

Raspberry gratin

SERVES 12

I think this dish is very special. It is made up of contrasts – sweet and sharp, soft and crisp, hot and cold. Basically, it is a lemon soufflé-type mixture set in individual moulds with a layer of raspberries in the centre.

12oz (350g) caster sugar
1 pack powdered gelatine
5 fl oz (140ml) double cream
5 fl oz (140ml) lemon juice
1oz (30g) cornflour
10 egg yolks (size-2 eggs)
7 egg whites (size-2 eggs)
9oz (250g) fresh raspberries
icing sugar

1. Place 10oz (275g) caster sugar with 6 fl oz (170ml) cold water in a medium-sized pan. Bring to the boil, stirring gently until the sugar dissolves. Boil rapidly until 5 fl oz (140ml) of sugar syrup remains.
2. Measure 3 fl oz (90ml) of cold water into a cup, sprinkle the gelatine on to it and stir with a teaspoon. Place in a pan containing enough water to come halfway up the sides of the cup and simmer until the gelatine has dissolved. Remove from the heat but leave the cup in the water.
3. Pour the cream into a pan. Measure out the lemon juice and use a little to 'slake' the cornflour in a little ramekin. Add to the cream, along with the remaining lemon juice. Bring to the boil whisking with a balloon whisk, and, once thickened, continue to cook for 2 minutes. Add the yolks all at once and whisk together over a medium heat until the mixture becomes thick. Don't worry – at this stage it looks curdled but it will be alright.
4. Set a sieve over a bowl and empty the mixture into it and press through. Use a bowl scraper to remove every scrap from the pan and from the base of the sieve. Add the gelatine and gently mix together. (The gelatine should still be hot enough to feel hot if you dip your little finger into it.)
5. At this stage, or earlier, line a tray with waxed paper and place 12 rings on it as close as you like – I use black-and-red non-stick rings, $3^1/4$in. (10cm) diameter, $1^1/4$in. (4cm) high, which are sold as muffin rings.
6. Place the whites in a spotlessly clean bowl. Whisk, using a hand-held or free-

standing mixer, until lightly whipped. Gradually add the remaining $2^1/_2$oz (65g) caster sugar while continuing to whisk. Once the mixture is softly 'peaky', start to pour in the hot sugar syrup in a slow stream. Continue whisking until a dense, stiff consistency is formed. Don't overdo it though, as the whites will become dry and lumpy – I know, I've been there.

7. Whisk a quarter of this into the lemon mixture, then fold in the remainder. Using a ladle or large spoon, half-fill each ring mould. Arrange about 8 raspberries on top, then cover with the remainder. Smooth over with a palette knife so that it is level with the top of the rings. Refrigerate until needed. I normally make them the day before.

8. 30 minutes before serving, preheat the grill so that it becomes very hot. Check beforehand which height you will need to slide the rings in at – you want them to be as close to the heat as possible. Lay out heatproof serving plates – I use little white, eared, Aplico ones which can withstand the high temperature. Please don't ruin your best china.

9. Slide a fish slice under the ring, transfer on to the dish, then run a knife around the inside edge of the ring. Lift off and repeat with the desired number. Sieve icing sugar over the top – enough to cover but not too thick. Place on a heatproof tray and place under the grill. Have underplates ready to put them on to, to make serving easier. Don't go away at this stage – watch them like a hawk as they burn quickly. The sugar should turn into an even, golden, crisp caramel. Remove, place on an underplate and serve straight away – they don't like waiting around.

CHAPTER THREE

RONNIE CLYDESDALE

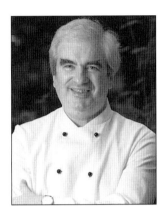

I HAVE childhood memories of my mother making broth using flank of beef from the nine-hole: it had to be nine-hole. The family shared the soup but my father had the beef as his main course. We children probably thought it too fatty anyway but he loved it served with root vegetables, Ayrshire potatoes and mustard freshly made from the powder.

It is not such a big step from this simple peasant meal to poaching fillet steak in an intense broth and using the same broth to cook the veg, as we do with *Scotch fillet of beef poached in root vegetables and served with barley risotto and an Arran-grain-mustard vinaigrette.*

Scottish cooking, both Highland and Lowland, has a tradition of cooking pot-au-feu style. In a Michelin-starred restaurant in Lyons I was delighted to see the chef create a dish from neck of lamb, rice and vegetables all cooked in a stock, the soup providing the starter, and the main course comprising the strained solids served with spicy sauces and dips. How Scottish, and how my father would have enjoyed and recognised such a dish.

The only proviso in poaching the meat is that you have to use a boiling broth. This has the same effect as searing meat under a grill or in the frying-pan. And if you use a cheaper cut of meat, the boiling has a tendering effect – plunging meat into boiling water is, in any case, an old butcher's trick for tenderising meat.

This type of cooking is very successful with steak. For a start, the meat doesn't dry out the way it could in a frying-pan. The other great advantage of poaching is that the meat does not really shrink. If you fry or grill an 8oz steak, what ends up on your plate is a 5–6oz steak. But putting the meat into boiling broth produces very little shrinkage.

53

In developing the dish, I wanted to retain the traditional element throughout. I had thought of using the barley straight out of the broth but that would not be very interesting. Finally, I hit upon the idea of making the barley into a risotto, which can also be sharpened with the addition of vinaigrette.

Three hundred years ago in Scotland, the well-heeled would have turned their noses up at lamb. It wasn't considered to have much flavour. Mutton was the thing. And mutton stuffed with seafood was ubiquitous. The origin of *Scotch mutton stuffed with mussels with a white-wine-and-shellfish sauce* goes back as far as the traditional cooking of the seventeenth century. In those days, the mutton would have been stuffed with oysters rather than mussels. Strange though it may seem, this was not to give the dish any upmarket appeal. On the contrary, oysters were so common that it was actually a way of making the dish less expensive.

It has also been something of a tradition to mix shellfish and meat, something which the Scots share with the French. I know of no such tradition in English cooking. Chicken and beef can also be used with shellfish, but mutton provides the best complement of flavours. Mutton these days has a poor image, which is a shame because the flavour is very intense. Find a good butcher.

I opened the Ubiquitous Chip 23 years ago in a back alley in Glasgow's West End. Prior to this, I worked in the Scotch whisky industry, and one of the perks of this employment was a fair amount of dining out. I began to notice that my hosts, who entertained maybe six times a week, pressed me to have the smoked salmon crevettes stuffed with prawns and Marie Rose sauce while they were inquiring about anything home-made and wholesome.

I came to agree with them. These were the days of flambé cooking, of wine bottles pushed into daft wee wicker baskets, of French menus with subtitles, of food without provenance and of little character and quite bland and forgettable within the hour.

I knew of no restaurant attempting to develop the Scots tradition, and nobody cared very much where ingredients came from. My first menu carried Oban-landed squid and was categorised by a customer as a 'fun menu' because everybody knew squid came from Barcelona or somewhere.

RONNIE CLYDESDALE has won many awards for his cooking, and the Ubiquitous Chip Wine Shop, which is next door, has won as many awards for its wine operation. The recipes which appear in this chapter are taken from *The Ubiquitous Chip Recipe Book*, published by Reed.

Barley risotto with olive-oil crostini

SERVES 4

This is a thoroughly Scottish dish, using pearl barley rather than rice for the risotto. This dish is very simple to cook. It is obviously an excellent dish for vegetarians. It can be served as a starter or as an accompaniment to a main course such as Scotch fillet of beef poached in root vegetables (see page 60). Equally, the crostini can be served as a starter on its own.

12 black olives
a few capers
fresh parsley
2 slices bread
extra-virgin olive oil
1 small sweet red pepper
1 small red onion
3lb (1.35kg) cultivated mushrooms
3 fl oz (75ml) olive oil
6oz (175g) pearl barley
$^2/_3$pt (400ml) water
6oz (175g) varied wild mushrooms
fresh tarragon
few drops of tamari (optional)
1 fl oz (25ml) medium sherry, preferably Amontillado

1. For the crostini, stone and rinse the olives, rinse the capers and chop the parsley.
2. Cut the bread into 8 discs of $1^1/_2$in. (4cm) diameter. Paint with olive oil.
3. Bake the bread in the oven until crisp.
4. Remove the skin from the pepper – this can be done by grilling or roasting or even by use of a blowlamp.
5. Finely chop the vegetable ingredients. Dress them with olive oil and pile on the discs of bread.
6. Make a mushroom stock with the cultivated mushrooms. Quarter or slice the mushrooms and stew in about 1oz of olive oil until the exuded liquor evaporates.
7. Add the water and cook until it reduces by half and the resulting stock is intensely flavoured with mushroom.

8.   For the risotto, wash and drain the barley.
9.   Place the drained barley with the remaining oil in an oven tray and fry on top of the stove until the barley takes on a good, rich colour.
10. While the barley is still cooking on top of the stove, add the strained mushroom stock.
11. Add 5oz (150g) of the wild mushrooms, tarragon, tamari and sherry into the barley.
12. Cover and simmer for 15 minutes, shaking to prevent sticking.
13. Lightly fry the remaining 1oz (25g) of wild mushrooms with a sprig of tarragon.
14. Finish the barley in a low oven (200°F/100°C) for 5–10 minutes. The barley grains should be separate but tender and have absorbed all the mushroom stock.

To serve the dish
Place 2 crostini on each plate and divide the barley equally. Garnish with the lightly fried wild mushroom and tarragon.

Scotch salmon in dill and whisky

SERVES 6

*This is quite a different way of serving salmon. You can try it as below or with
variations such as with mayonnaise into which you have mixed a little grain
mustard; with mollet egg; or with the skin of the salmon chopped and crisped
under a hot grill and sprinkled over scrambled egg.*

$1^{1}/_{2}$oz (40g) coarse sea-salt
1 level tsp freshly ground black pepper
$1^{1}/_{2}$oz (40g) demerara sugar
1oz (25ml) of whisky. (I prefer malt from the west coast of Islay redolent of
    peat and seaweed)
plenty of fresh dill weed

1. Mix the salt, pepper, sugar and whisky to a thick paste.
2. Cover the base of a suitably sized tray with dill and place a fillet, skin-side
   down, on top. Smear the exposed flesh with the whisky mix and cover with
   dill.
3. Repeat this process with the second fillet and place it on top of the other,
   skin-side up. Cover with dill – it is difficult to use too much dill in this
   recipe.
4. Place a tray on top and weigh down using a couple of heavy plates. Keep in a
   cold place for 24 hours, turning the fillets a couple of times. The fish should
   keep well for several days, and you can have arguments over whether it
   actually improves with age.

To serve the dish
Scrupulously scrape off the dill and spices and cut into thin slices. Present and
serve as you would smoked salmon.

Scotch mutton stuffed with mussels with a white-wine-and-shellfish sauce

SERVES 12

This very traditional Scottish dish produces a perfect complement of flavours. There's plenty of good eating, too, and the dish is relatively simple to prepare.

4lb of mussels
1 gigot of mutton – approximately $7^{1}/_{2}$lb (3.3kg)
diced vegetables – carrots, turnips, celery and onion
shellfish for stock – talk to your fishmonger. Prawns, langoustines and small
   crabs are ideal, and it is sometimes possible to have the shells for the asking
2oz brandy
1 bottle dry white wine – Vouvray is ideal
juice and zest of lemon
twine

1. Wash and de-beard mussels in cold water. Discard any that remain open – reserve 2 dozen for final garnish.
2. Open mussels by cooking in a dry frying-pan and discard any that refuse to open. Discard also the juices exuded from the mussels as they are too salty for our purpose. Remove meat from shells.
3. Bone out the gigot, roast the bone in oven at 475°F/240°C/Gas Mark 9 for 10–15 minutes with the vegetables until the bone takes on colour.
4. Transfer to a stock pot, add bouquet garni, cover with cold water and simmer for several hours, topping up the water as necessary.
5. Break or pulverise the shellfish and fry in a clean pot in a little oil for 5 minutes to extract maximum flavour.
6. Deglaze pot with brandy, then add the strained liquor from the mutton stock.
7. Simmer for 20 minutes, strain, then add the bottle of wine.
8. Trim excess fat from mutton and place skin-side down.
9. Line the topside with the mussel meat, sprinkle with lemon juice, season, roll up and tie with twine at 1in. ($2^{1}/_{2}$cm) intervals.
10. Place mutton in an oven dish and cover with the completed stock. Cover with foil and cook for $1^{1}/_{2}$ hours in a medium oven.
11. Remove meat from tray and keep warm. Reduce the cooking liquid until it coats the back of a spoon.
12. Open remainder of mussels. Slice meat thickly.

To serve the dish

Place two slices of mutton on each dinner plate. Place mussels at top of picture and sauce at bottom. Samphire is wonderful with this dish as both garnish and as a part of the stuffing but is extremely difficult to obtain. An alternative garnish would be lemon zest blanched for 4 minutes in boiling water and caramelised by dropping zest in a demerara sugar syrup cooked to soft-ball stage – like toffee apples. Remove zest with a slotted spoon to a cold plate and separate by using your fingers dipped in icy water.

Scotch fillet of beef poached in root vegetables and served with barley risotto and Arran-grain-mustard vinaigrette.

SERVES 6

This is a wonderful way to cook beef, with the meat taking flavour from the vegetable broth. It's also very simple to do and more economic than frying or grilling beef.

syboes tops cut off 1in. (2^1/$_2$cm) above bulb
diced carrots, turnips, onions, celery
plenty of beef bones for broth
bay leaves, thyme
6 fillet steaks, each 6–8oz (175–225g)
barley risotto (see page 55)
vinaigrette (see below)

1. Reserve syboes bulbs and enough of the other vegetables to serve with your completed dish.
2. Put remainder of the vegetables with the syboes tops and beef bones in the oven until they take colour. Transfer to a large pot, cover with water, add bay leaves and thyme, bring to boil then simmer forever or until every scrap of flavour and protein has been extracted from bones. You need stock of real power.
3. Strain into a clean pot and reduce until you have an intensely flavoured broth.
4. Now poach your reserved vegetables in broth, until they are cooked but retain a firmness. Remove and keep warm.
5. With your broth at a rolling boil, plunge in steaks and allow them to cook for 10 minutes – they should be pink. Remove to warm place to rest but keep the broth boiling as you go about the assembly.

Vinaigrette

1 tsp Arran grain mustard
2oz (50g) red-wine vinegar
6oz (175g) sunflower oil

Whisk the mustard into the red-wine vinegar, add oil and keep
whisking until it is quite emulsified.

To serve the dish

Place steak on dinner plate, put a mound of vegetables on one side and the
barley risotto on the other. Ladle some of the scalding and, by now, very beefy
broth over the steak and the vegetables. Offer the vinaigrette as an optional
dressing for the risotto. Do not garnish. The leftover broth is a wonderful
soup, good enough to enliven the dreichest Saturday watching Partick Thistle.

Turbot or halibut in a green-peppercorn-and-pine-kernel crust with a red-wine-and-chocolate sauce

SERVES 6

This is a great fish and a great dish, and the peppercorns and kernels add a lively texture and flavour.

2 red onions
1 bottle red wine
2 carrots
6 black peppercorns
parsley
2 tbsp sunflower oil
1 tbsp red-wine vinegar
$1^{1}/_{2}$pt (900ml) water
bouquet garni of thyme, parsley, bay leaf and celery top
turbot/halibut carcase of trimmings, head and bones
6oz (175g) of combined wholewheat and white breadcrumbs
3 tbsp broken pine kernels
$1^{1}/_{2}$oz (40g) rinsed green peppercorns
6 fillet of turbot or halibut, each 6–8oz (175–225g)
1 cube Bournville dark or other good chocolate
sea-salt

1. To make the stock for the red-wine-and-chocolate sauce, slice red onions and carrots and crush black peppercorns. Chop some parsley and set aside for the topping. Also set aside some unchopped parsley.
2. Fry onions in 1 tbsp sunflower oil until they take on a little colour – do not burn. Add carrots.
3. Add red wine, water, bouquet garni, red-wine vinegar, crushed peppercorns and turbot carcase of trimmings, head and bones.
4. Bring to the boil, then reduce to simmer for 30 minutes.
5. Strain and allow to cool.
6. Strain into clean pot and bring to the boil.
7. Reduce the stock until it has achieved a coating consistency.
8. Remove from direct heat and retain at just below boiling point.
9. In a frying-pan, make a topping by frying together the wholewheat and white crumbs, pine kernels, green peppercorns, sea salt, 1 tbsp sunflower oil and

chopped parsley. Fry until crumbs are golden.

10. Now put the fillets of turbot or halibut in a tight dish – but make sure the fillets do not overlap each other.

11. Pour in the stock, cover and bring gently to the boil for 2 minutes.

12. Remove fish and reserve.

13. Preheat oven to maximum temperature.

14. Put the crumbs on top of each fillet to form a coating.

15. Brush an oven dish lightly with oil, place fillets on top and put uncovered in fierce oven for 2–3 minutes until fish is perfectly cooked and crust is formed.

16. Deep fry the unchopped parsley.

17. Beat the cube of chocolate into the hot sauce – the chocolate should lend an unctuousness to the sauce but not overwhelm the taste.

To serve the dish

Pour sauce on to hot serving plate. Place fillet in the middle. Garnish with deep-fried parsley.

Scotch-whisky tart

SERVES 10

We first prepared this dish for the Macallan Whisky company and used this magnificent nectar to fatten the raisins. On another occasion two Italian guests returned the morning after dinner complete with carry-out pizza boxes and had us bake four to take home to mother.

8oz (225g) (dry weight) raisins
whisky – enough of your favourite brand to cover the raisins in a bowl
6oz (175g) plain flour
3oz (75g) caster sugar
4oz (100–125g) unsalted butter
1 egg
5 eggs, beaten
1pt (600ml) double cream
juice of a lemon
$\frac{1}{4}$ of a grated nutmeg
$\frac{1}{2}$ tsp cinnamon
$\frac{1}{4}$ ground clove

1. Steep the raisins overnight in the whisky.
2. To make the pastry, process the flour, butter and sugar until it takes on a fine crumb texture. Blend in the egg and remove to fridge to rest.
3. Gently mix together the beaten eggs with the cream, lemon juice, nutmeg, cinnamon and clove and add any unabsorbed whisky from the raisins.
4. Roll out pastry and line a well-buttered – you must use unsalted butter – 12in. (30cm) flan ring. Return to fridge to set. Cover base of pastry with foil, add dried beans to prevent pastry from rising and bake blind for 10 minutes in a preheated oven at 150°C/300°F/Gas Mark 2.
5. Allow to cool slightly. Remove beans and foil and paint base with lightly beaten egg white.
6. Pour the fat raisins over the base of the flan, then gently add the egg mixture. Bake uncovered in a preheated oven at 150°C/300°F/Gas Mark 2 until set – 45 minutes.

CHAPTER FOUR

FRANCES ATKINS

FOR years, people have been trying to guess the secret ingredient of my *minted-pea-and-bean flan.* Even John Tovey, writing his recipe column for the *Radio Times*, got it wrong. He worked out the rest of the recipe, but couldn't work out my secret. The secret ingredient is Philadelphia cheese because it holds the peas together. It has to be Philadelphia and not any other kind of cream cheese because of its texture.

The dish has always been a big favourite, but it has an interesting history. At one time in Farleyer House in Perthshire, we grew all our own vegetables, which turned out to be a useless exercise because the rabbits got them. But, of course, we had to find uses for our home-grown peas and lovely broad beans. The original concept was a mousse with Parmesan in the pastry. But I didn't like the texture of the mousse; I thought it was too rich. So then I tried the idea out as a terrine. But I thought that was a bit boring. Finally, I came upon the idea of the flan and using Philadelphia rather than Parmesan.

Now I do a lot of vegetarian dishes. I think there is a female way of looking at food: cooking that is gutsy but light, that doesn't leave you feeling bloated. Women want to eat well without putting on weight, and female chefs aim to help their customers achieve that. That's the difference between male and female chefs – women tend to think about their customers, while men tend to think about their skills as a chef.

I'm an enormous fan of game. It's one of the great joys of cooking in Scotland – there is so much game, and so fresh, the best quality. When I first cooked in Scotland, I tried all kinds of game. Venison is my favourite game, good wild venison, especially roe deer, which is a lovely meat because it's dense. It was when I had cooked venison and all the game birds and was looking for something else that was wild that I came up with the idea of using hare. I hadn't cooked hare when I was in Buckinghamshire because people were scared of using it. There was a certain squeamishness about cooking hare because in order to get a good finish you have to use the blood and guts to thicken the sauce. I tend to come up with complete dishes. I think of a food and what could go with it, bearing in mind colour as well as texture and taste.

With my *baked hare with mustard, pears, endive and watercress* I was thinking of autumn, something rustic. I was thinking about what would be in season and go with the meat. The pear part came from thinking that pears are at their best in autumn. The sweetness of poached pear complements the rich meat of the hare. The watercress adds a peppery flavour. The soufflé potatoes are an interesting addition, much better than something like olive-oil mashed potato, which would be too heavy for the dish. The only note about this dish is you have to use wild hare because, unlike rabbit, the tame ones aren't very good.

It's a trait of mine to cook fruit with game. Prunes seemed the ideal combination when I was thinking of how to cook teal, which is baby duck. The great thing about this *roast teal with prunes, leek and teal parfait* is you're cooking a whole bird, so you get excellent results, and it's a nice portion size. Prunes were my first choice for teal. When I'm thinking about fruit with game, I'm thinking of my own taste buds. I cook to satisfy myself. What would I enjoy?

FRANCES ATKINS opened Shaws Restaurant in Old Brompton Rd in London last year. Prior to that, with her husband, Bill, she had transformed Farleyer House in Perthshire into a top country-house hotel acclaimed for its cooking. She is a founder member of the Scottish Chefs Association and serves on its Advisory Board.

Essentially a self-taught chef, Frances worked in the Box Tree in Yorkshire and ran her own outside-catering business in Buckinghamshire before opening Atkins Restaurant with Bill in Great Missenden and later moving to larger premises nearby at the Old Plow in Speen.

Chicken-and-almond wafer with coriander-and-aubergine salsa with almond sugar

SERVES 4

In the restaurant, we serve this dish as a starter, but it is also useful as a canapé. The Moroccan spice for this recipe has so many other uses that you'll probably want to keep it in the kitchen as a general flavouring. The salsa can also be used with other dishes.

3 breasts of chicken
3 shallots
1 tsp fresh ginger
pinch of saffron stamens
1 fl oz (25ml) chicken stock
$^1/_2$oz (15g) butter
$^1/_2$ tsp garlic purée
2 tsp Moroccan spice mix (see recipe below)
ground black pepper
juice of 1 lime
2 small eggs
almond sugar (see recipe below)
1 pack filo pastry
melted butter (for brushing over pastry)
sesame seeds
$^1/_2$pt (300ml) strong chicken stock
rocket leaves

1. Cut the breasts of chicken into small strips. Finely chop the shallots, chop the fresh ginger. Infuse the saffron stamens in the chicken stock.
2. Make the Moroccan spice mix (see recipe below) and set to one side.
3. Make the almond sugar (see recipe below) and set to one side.
4. Sweat the chopped shallots in the butter, without allowing them to change colour.
5. Add ginger and garlic and slightly colour the mixture.
6. Add the chicken and Moroccan spice mix and black pepper.
7. Cook until the chicken is sealed.
8. Add the saffron, chicken stock and lime juice.
9. Bring to the boil for 2 minutes.

10. Take off the heat and place in a dish with a cover. Let it infuse until cold.
11. When cold, drain off the stock.
12. Place the stock in pan and boil until reduced by two-thirds.
13. Beat the 2 eggs and add to the stock. Cook as for scrambled egg on a very low heat until set.
14. Shred the chicken mixture and add to the scrambled egg and leave to cool.
15. When cool, add a pinch of almond sugar to the chicken.
16. Wrap the chicken mixture in rectangles of filo pastry parcels.
17. Brush with melted butter and dust with sesame seeds.
18. Cook on 400°F/200°C/Gas Mark 6 for approx. 10 minutes until the pastry is crisp and lightly coloured. Serve hot.

Almond sugar
8oz (225g) blanched sugar
4oz (100–125g) caster sugar
$^1/_2$ cinnamon stick
1oz almonds

1. Toast almonds with the cinnamon stick on a piece of foil under the grill.
2. While still hot, blend the mixture in processor with sugar. The resulting mixture should resemble rough crumbs.

Moroccan spice mix
1 tsp star anise
1 tsp fennel seeds
8 whole allspice berries
1 tsp ground cardamon
8 whole cloves
15 whole black peppercorns
1 stick cinnamon
1 tbsp sesame seeds
1 tsp ground coriander
$^1/_2$ tsp cumin
pinch of cayenne pepper
pinch of mace
1 tbsp ground ginger
1 tsp ground nutmeg

1. Mix all the ingredients together.
2. Chop until ground.

Coriander-and-aubergine salsa

2 aubergines
1 dessertspoon coriander seeds
4 shallots
4oz (100–125g) fresh coriander leaves
4oz (100–125g) sundried tomatoes in oil

1. Peel the aubergines, finely chop the coriander seeds and shallots, chop the fresh coriander.
2. Roast aubergines in a little oil from the tomatoes until soft.
3. Cool the aubergines and then dice them.
4. Sweat off the shallots.
5. Dice the tomatoes.
6. Mix in the other ingredients and season to taste with salt and pepper.

To serve the dish

Lay the almond wafer in the middle of the plate. Arrange the salsa around the almond wafer. Serve with the rocket leaves.

Asparagus, parsley and saffron risotto

SERVES 2

This is a very interesting vegetarian dish which can be served both as a starter and a main course.

1 dessertspoon finely chopped parsley
4 finely chopped shallots
6 asparagus
pinch of saffron stamens
5 fl oz (150ml) white wine (medium, not too dry)
8 fl oz (225ml) vegetable stock
3 fl oz (75ml) olive oil
4oz (100–125g) aborio rice
2oz (50g) butter
2oz (50g) Parmesan cheese

1. Finely chop the parsley and the shallots.
2. Cut off the asparagus tips, which should be left whole. Chop up the rest of the asparagus.
3. Cook the asparagus tips in salted water.
4. Put the cooked asparagus to one side.
5. Infuse the saffron stamens in the white wine and the vegetable stock.
6. Warm the oil and sweat off the shallots. Add the rice and cook until rice is semi-soft.
7. Stir the mixture well. Add the saffron liquid and cook until the rice has absorbed the liquid.
8. Add the chopped ends of asparagus, the chopped parsley and the butter.
9. Season with salt and pepper to taste.

To serve the dish
Serve with the fresh Parmesan cheese.

Minted-pea-and-bean flan

SERVES 4

This is an ideal starter, but it can be served as a main course.

7in. (18cm) approx. tin lined with shortcrust pastry (see recipe below)
4 leaves of gelatine
4 fl oz (125ml) white wine
1lb (450g) fresh shelled peas (not frozen)
4oz (100–125g) Philadelphia cheese
4oz (100–125g) mayonnaise
1 bunch of fresh mint (approx. 4 stems with the leaves picked off), chopped
$^{3}/_{4}$oz (20g) sugar
4 fl oz (125ml) whipped cream
broad beans or haricot vert

1. Make shortcrust pastry (see recipe below), soften gelatine in white wine.
2. Cook shelled peas. Place cooked peas in food processor with Philadelphia cheese and stir in mayonnaise and the melted gelatine and wine.
3. Pass the processed mixture through a sieve, and mix in chopped mint and sugar.
4. Fold in cream, place in pastry case and refrigerate until set.
5. Cook peeled broad beans or haricot vert and serve with dish.

Shortcrust pastry
13oz (375g) plain flour
$^{1}/_{2}$oz (15g) salt
8oz (225g) unsalted butter
4oz (100–125g) grated fresh Parmesan
1 beaten egg
2fl oz (50ml) cold water

1. Sieve flour and salt into bowl, add diced butter and add to flour and salt.
2. Rub flour into butter until like breadcrumbs, add Parmesan.
3. Add the beaten egg and cold water and bake blind together gently.
4. Wrap in cling film, refrigerate for 2 hours before use, then bring to room temperature. Roll out, line flan tin and bake blind.
5. Cool before adding filling.

Turban of sea-bass, spinach and prawns with a broad-bean ragout

SERVES 1

I love fish, and in this dish the combination of prawns and sea-bass is particularly exciting. Because it is being served in a ramekin, the quantities are for one portion, but it is easy enough to serve to a number of guests by using several ramekins. The quantities for the ragout would need to increase accordingly, but you will have enough fish velouté to serve as the base for a ragout for more than one person.

melted butter
1 small sea-bass fillet, approx. 5–6oz (150–175g), skinned
3oz (75g) well-drained spinach
2oz (50g) raw, uncooked prawns
$^1/_2$ egg white
salt
2fl oz (50ml) cream
1oz (25g) cooked prawns, chopped
3oz (75g) broad beans
2 or 3 button shallots
new potatoes
fish velouté (see recipe below)

1. Line a No. 2 ramekin dish with cling film, leaving plenty of overlap.
2. Brush the cling film with melted butter.
3. Line the sea-bass fillet inside the ramekin dish and season lightly.
4. Chop the spinach and cook it.
5. Now place the uncooked prawns in the food processor with the egg white and salt. Add cream. Remove from processor and add chopped, cooked prawns and chopped, cooked spinach. This will provide you with a mousse mixture.
6. Place the mousse on top of the sea-bass in the ramekin.
7. Cover with overlap of cling film and cook in the microwave on half-power for approx. 2 minutes.
8. Cook the broad beans, shallots and new potatoes in the normal way.

Fish velouté
8 shallots
$^1/_2$oz (15g) unsalted butter
16fl oz (475ml) dry white wine
10fl oz (300ml) dry sherry
1pt (600ml) fish stock
8fl oz (225g) cream
salt/pepper

1. Finely chop the shallots and sweat them in the butter until they are softened but have not changed colour.
2. Add white wine and sherry to the pan and reduce by two-thirds until you have a syrup.
3. Add fish stock and reduce a little until it amalgamates with the rice.
4. Add the cream and reduce to a coating consistency to hold the broad beans, button shallots and new potatoes.

To serve the dish
Serve on the plate as a ragout with the fish velouté around the ramekin.

Roast teal with prunes, leek and teal parfait

SERVES 1

This is an excellent dish for cooking at home for a dinner party because you could cook one teal per person. The dish is really quite straightforward. The flavour of the teal goes very well with the leek and the teal-liver parfait. Your butcher will be able to provide teal. You will have enough sauce for several portions and the recipe for teal parfait will work with more than one teal liver – just increase the ingredients in proportion.

2 prunes
4fl oz (100ml) port
1 teal (baby duck)
2oz (50g) teal parfait (see recipe below)
1 slice of brioche or bread
1 large chopped leek
teal sauce (see recipe below)
2fl oz (50ml) cream
4 green peppercorns
half a rasher of bacon

1. The night before, place the prunes in the port and leave to marinate overnight.
2. Remove liver from teal to make teal parfait (see recipe below).
3. Seal the teal breast-on in the frying pan with oil and seasoning. Pop the teal the other way around on baking tray in the oven at 425°F/220°C/Gas Mark 7 for 7 minutes.
4. Remove the teal from the oven, keep it warm and let it rest.
5. Cut a circle out of the brioche or bread and deep fry, being sure to drain well once fried.
6. Cover fried bread with teal parfait.
7. Cut leek into circles and cook.
8. Warm the prunes in the teal sauce (see recipe below).
9. Remove breasts from teal, taking the leg with it. The teal should be bleeding slightly and the meat relaxed. Place the bacon on top.

Teal parfait
1 shallot
1 rasher of bacon
1 teal liver
2oz (50g) chicken liver
4oz (100–125g) butter
1 tsp brandy
1 fl oz (25ml) cream

1. Chop the shallot and finely dice the bacon.
2. Sauté chopped shallot, dried bacon, teal liver, and chicken liver in 2oz (50g) butter until pink.
3. Add the brandy.
4. Place in food processor. Process until smooth. Add the rest of the butter. Add the cream. Add salt and pepper to taste.
5. Leave to cool, cover and leave to set in fridge.

Teal sauce
3 shallots
4fl oz (100ml) port
$^{1}/_{2}$pt (300ml) red wine
$^{1}/_{2}$pt (300ml) veal stock
4oz (100–125g) unsalted butter
1 tsp double cream
4 green peppercorns

1. Drain the prunes from the marinated port.
2. Finely chop and cook the shallots in a medium heat in the port, red wine and veal stock.
3. Reduce the mixture down to 4fl oz (100ml).
4. Whisk in the butter, cream, and add green peppercorns and the prunes.

To serve the dish
Place the fried bread on the plate with teal parfait on top. Put the cooked leek on top of that and the teal on top of the leek. Add cream to the teal sauce and serve over the dish. Ideally, this dish should be served with new potatoes which have been lightly sautéed whole.

Trio of chargrilled Mediterranean fish with roast vegetables and Thai sauce

SERVES 4

This is a very quick dish to cook, and, being full of colour, it presents very well. The Thai sauce gives it a delicate lift and can be used for other dishes.

Thai sauce (see recipe below)
1 carrot
1 parsnip
1 fennel
1 aubergine
1 red pepper
1 courgette
6fl oz (175ml) good Tuscan olive oil
salt and pepper
1 small fillet of red mullet
1 small fillet of sea-bass
1 small fillet of John Dory

1. Make Thai sauce (see recipe below).
2. Wash the carrot, parsnip and fennel. Peel these vegetables and cut them into slices on the slant. Blanch them in hot water and refresh them in cold water.
3. Slice the aubergine on the slant.
4. De-seed the pepper and cut on the slant. Cut courgette on the slant.
5. Toss the vegetables in the olive oil and season with salt and pepper.
6. Roast the vegetables, lightly smeared in olive oil, for approx. 10 minutes.
7. While they are roasting, heat a riveted non-stick pan on the top of the stove.
8. Now oil and season your fish.
9. When the non-stick pan is very hot, grill the fish until crisp on both sides. Season.

Thai sauce

$1^{1}/_{2}$oz (40g) root ginger
1 stalk lemongrass
2 red chillies
2 cloves of garlic
2 tsp chopped fresh coriander
4oz (100–125g) melted butter
$^{1}/_{4}$tsp green peppercorns
5fl oz (150ml) fish stock
5fl oz (150ml) sweetish white wine
2 tsp lime juice
$^{1}/_{2}$tsp ground coriander
10fl oz (300ml) coconut milk
salt and pepper

1. Finely chop root ginger, lemongrass and red chillies. Crush garlic. Chop fresh coriander.
2. Melt butter and sauté ginger, garlic, peppercorns, lemongrass and chillies.
3. Add fish stock, white wine, lime juice and coriander. Add coconut milk gradually and bring to the boil. Reduce heat and simmer for 8–10 minutes.
4. Cool slightly.
5. Place in liquidiser.
6. Once liquidised, pass through sieve.
7. Warm the sauce, stir in the coriander leaves and season to taste.

To serve the dish

Place the vegetables in a pile on the plate with the fish on top. Spoon Thai sauce over the top.

Baked hare with mustard, pears, endive and watercress

SERVES 4

This dish is one of marvellous contrasts and succulent flavours. The saddle of the hare is served almost raw, while the leg is well cooked. The pears add sweetness and the watercress a peppery flavour. I usually serve this dish with soufflé potatoes.

2 carrots
1 onion
2 stalks of celery
1 fennel
1 wild skinned hare
1 dessertspoon tomato purée
4 black peppercorns
2 bay leaves
4 juniper berries
1pt (600ml) red wine
1fl oz (25ml) game stock
watercress and endive for salad
hazelnut oil
1 pear
sugar syrup – $^3/_4$pt (450ml) water and 1lb (450g) sugar
1 dessertspoon ready-mixed English mustard
salt

1. Finely chop and sauté the vegetables and place to one side.
2. Remove the two fillets running across the saddle and place to one side.
3. Remove the legs.
4. Sauté the legs and the carcase in oil along with the mirepoix of vegetables until legs, carcase and vegetables are all well browned.
5. Add the tomato purée, peppercorns, bay leaves, juniper berries, red wine and game stock.
6. Bake in a medium oven at 350°F/180°C/Gas Mark 4 for approx. 50 minutes until tender.
7. While this is cooking, make a salad of the watercress and endive, dress with hazelnut oil, and place to one side.
8. When you have made the salad, poach a pear in sugar syrup for 15 minutes.

9. Remove the dish from the oven and let the dish cool. Remove the leg meat from the bone and remove the carcase altogether.
10. Strain the remaining liquid into the mustard. Check seasoning and bring to the boil.
11. Add the hare's blood and guts to the mixture and strain immediately.
12. Quickly sauté the fillets until they are very pink.
13. Slice the fillets thinly.

To serve the dish

Place the leg meat on the plate and pour the sauce over it. Place the thinly sliced fillets on top of the leg meat. Serve with the poached pear and the salad.

Chocolate tart

SERVES 6

I claim no credit for this delicious chocolate tart, which was created by my sous chef, Neil. This chocolate tart needs to be thin rather than thick, otherwise it is too rich. We serve this with caramelised oranges and crème fraîche.

11oz (300g) chocolate
4oz (100–125g) butter
4fl oz (100ml) single cream
vanilla essence
dark rum
4 eggs
1 egg yolk
4oz (100–125g) sugar
sable-paste pastry case (see recipe below)

1. Prepare a pre-baked pastry case approx. 12in. (300cm) diameter (see recipe below).
2. Gently melt chocolate, butter and cream into a bowl.
3. Add vanilla essence and rum to taste.
4. Whisk eggs, yolk and sugar to a light sabayon.
5. Fold in chocolate mix to the sabayon gently so as not to knock the air out.
6. Pour mix into pre-baked case and cook at 350°F/180°C/Gas Mark 4 until it is just setting on the surface.
7. Allow to cool.

Sable-paste pastry case
1lb (450g) butter
14oz (400g) icing sugar
6 eggs
$2^{1}/_{4}$lb (1kg) plain flour
4oz (100–125g) ground almonds

1. Cream the butter and sugar together.
2. Add the eggs gradually with a handful of flour to prevent splitting.
3. Add ground almonds, then the rest of the flour.
4. Rest well in fridge before use.

Frances Atkins
TRIO OF CHARGRILLED MEDITERRANEAN FISH WITH ROAST VEGETABLES AND THAI SAUCE

Nick Nairn

STRAWBERRY PAVLOVA WITH RASPBERRY SAUCE

CHAPTER FIVE

NICK NAIRN

I'VE been a soup fan since I was a kid. I find something heartening and comforting in soups. It's only now I realise how good the food I had as a kid was. I lived in the country with lots of salmon, venison and pheasant, but all plainly done, no sauces. Now, after eight years of running my own restaurant, I find that I'm looking to create food that is simpler with less artifice. I couldn't do soups properly when I started out. I'd been trying to use flour and things like potato to get consistency. Hilary Brown at La Potiniere was my inspiration. I remember having a red-pepper soup there that had a really intense flavour with vibrant colour, and I resolved to make better soups.

Carrot, honey and ginger soup was the first soup I'd made that I felt was any good. I'd started out making a carrot-and-coriander soup that had a lovely thick texture and colour. I started playing about with it and hit upon the idea of honey and ginger. It's like all good cooking: the things that turn you on are dead simple.

Most people are very surprised to hear that I cook a dish called *fillet of cod with mashed potato and spring onion and a caviar-butter sauce*. Cod is a very underrated fish because most people don't get to eat proper cod. What most people buy is cod fillets in which the flavour has mostly been washed out by the processing. Filleted properly, it's a wonderful fish – all those big thick flakes.

I started off making a fish pie after having eaten one at Gidleigh Park. My concept then was simply mashed potato with cod on top. But the first time I did it was a last-minute thing for Sunday lunch, and I added a herb-butter sauce. That seemed to be a good idea because all the plates came back licked clean. Then I started adding spring onion through the mashed potato. The mashed potato had first of all been all-butter, and then I was happier with a mixture of butter and olive oil. The caviar was a touch of inspiration. It really made people sit up and notice, and when I cooked it at last year's Scottish Food Proms Gala Dinner in Glasgow for 250 people it certainly caused a stir.

It doesn't really need caviar, though. The main thing is the mash has to be really good, sitting there like a shimmering quenelle, and the cod has to be translucent, not overcooked.

I hate fussy puddings. My cooking is all to do with eating. First it's flavour, then texture and temperature, and way down the line is visual presentation. But good food looks good unintentionally. If you get the food technically correct, then the visual usually follows.

I did *strawberry pavlova with raspberry sauce* when I first opened the restaurant, and at first it wasn't great to look at because traditionally pavlova is round. Then I had the idea to present it square, and that has made it much more interesting. I try to get the texture of the meringue as near to a marshmallow as I can.

One of the essential criteria for me in puddings is that they have to be easy to do. Then, because they are simple, I want them to be outstanding. So I take a simple idea and refine it technically. The result is a clean, simple, uncluttered pudding that tastes terrific.

NICK NAIRN was the youngest Scottish chef ever to win a Michelin star. A former merchant seaman, he is a self-taught chef and opened Braeval Old Mill with his wife, Fiona, in 1986. He has won many awards and appeared on television and radio. He also runs a cookery school at Braeval. He is a founder member of the Scottish Chefs Association and serves on its Advisory Board.

Carrot, honey and ginger soup

SERVES 6

Soups are a personal passion, especially this kind of puréed vegetable soup. The fact that they don't require any stock, are very easy to make, freeze well and are relatively cheap is secondary to their sublime, clean flavour and vibrant colour. Virtually any vegetables may be used with this method, root vegetables being particularly good. The secret is to cook the soups for the minimum time and chill immediately after liquidising and then reheat to order. They keep for three days in the fridge and six weeks in the freezer.

5oz (150g) onion
$^3/_4$oz (20g) bruised root ginger
3oz (75g) unsalted butter
1oz (25g) honey
21oz (600g) carrots
1$^1/_2$pt (1l) boiling water
$^1/_3$oz (8g) salt
$^1/_5$oz (5g) ground white pepper
$^1/_6$oz (4ml) lemon juice

1. Thinly slice the onions. Sweat the onions and ginger in the butter for 10 minutes – do not brown.
2. Stir in the honey and let it melt.
3. Add the carrots. Stir to coat the carrots and pour in enough boiling water to cover.
4. Add seasoning and bring to the boil on a high heat.
5. Simmer for 45 minutes until the vegetables are tender.
6. Pour into a liquidiser and process to a purée.
7. Check seasoning, add lemon juice and serve with a blob of cream.

Fettucine of roast red pepper, black olives and capers with pesto and rocket

SERVES 4

I love pasta, and this Mediterranean dish is a favourite. It is so easy to make and ideal for dinner parties as all the work is done in advance. Cooked, dried pasta is alright, but for the ultimate result go for fresh, home-made pasta.

1oz (25g) pesto (see recipe below)
2oz (60ml) sauce vierge (see recipe below)
1 x 5oz (160g) red pepper
16 best-quality black olives
8oz (240g) fresh cooked fettucine tagliatelle (see recipe below)
20 best-quality capers
$^2/_5$fl oz (10ml) lemon juice
$^2/_5$oz (10g) Maldon salt
$^1/_4$oz (6g) fresh-milled white pepper
$^4/_5$oz (20g) rocket leaves
$^3/_5$oz (15g) grated fresh Reggiano Parmesan

1. First of all you have to make 25g of pesto and 60ml of sauce vierge the night before (see recipes below).
2. Roast, skin and dice the red pepper.
3. Stone and quarter the black olives.
4. Mix the following ingredients together – the red pepper, the olives, the pasta, capers, lemon juice, Maldon salt, fresh-milled white pepper, rocket leaves, grated fresh Reggiano Parmesan, the pesto and the sauce vierge.
5. Place the mixture in a microwave dish. Cover with cling film and pierce film.
6. Microwave on high for 3 minutes.

Pesto

2oz (50g) basil leaves
1$^1/_2$oz (35g) fresh grated Reggiano Parmesan
1$^1/_2$oz (35g) pine kernels
1 clove of garlic
1$^1/_2$oz (5g) Maldon salt
3g fresh-milled black pepper
3fl oz (90ml) extra-virgin olive oil

Blitz all the ingredients together in a food processor.

Sauce vierge

2fl oz (60ml) first-cold-pressing extra-virgin olive oil
1oz (30g) very finely diced shallot
$^1/_2$ clove crushed garlic
1 sprig thyme

1. Combine all the ingredients and simmer over a very low heat for
   20 minutes.
2. Allow to infuse for 12 hours and then remove thyme and garlic.

Basic pasta dough

4oz (100–125g) plain flour
1 whole egg – size 3
1 egg yolk – size 3

1. Place the flour in a food processor and whizz, then add the eggs and
   allow the dough to work for 2–3 minutes. Tip out the dough and
   form into a ball shape, wrap in cling film and place in the fridge for 1
   hour before using.
2. To roll out the paste, cut the dough into 4 pieces and, using a rolling
   pin, flatten each ball. Fold over the dough and roll out several times
   until you have a rectangular shape.
3. With the pasta machine at its widest setting, start passing the pasta
   through the rollers, moving the rollers one step closer with each pass.
   On my machine I take the pasta down to the second thinnest
   position for most uses. Once you reach the desired thickness, pass the
   pasta through a second time at the same setting then allow to cool
   slightly before you do any of the following:
4. Cut out rounds or squares for lasagne. Pass through the big cutters
   for fettucine. Pass through the small cutter for tagliatelle. For

whichever size or shape you cut out, the pasta needs to be slightly dried before cooking – approximately 10 minutes over a broom handle seems about right.

5. To cook the pasta, have a large pot of boiling salted water ready, then drop in the pasta stirring until it comes back to the boil again. Cook for $2^1/_2$ minutes, then remove pasta with a slotted spoon or spaghetti fork and cool in a bowl of cold water.

6. Drain thoroughly and store in a tub for up to 12 hours before use. The pasta will stick together in the tub – to unstick it just add some water, give it a swirl round and drain again; the pasta will magically free itself.

PLEASE NOTE:
1. Do not add salt to the pasta dough, as this toughens it.
2. Do not add oil to the cooking pasta as it will not prevent sticking and is therefore a waste of oil.
3. Do not dredge the pasta in flour to prevent sticking as this will cause a gluey consistency when the pasta is cooked.

To serve the dish
Divide the mixture between 4 plates. Garnish with a julienne of fresh basil.

Lasagne of monkfish and mussels with spinach, tomato and saffron

SERVES 4

This is more complicated but well worth the effort. Organisation and pre-planning are the key. Cook the mussels and the pasta during the day. Have everything to hand for the plating, making sure that the plates or bowls are hot. Work as quickly and efficiently as possible. You really need two pairs of hands for the last bit, but practising on understanding friends will give you the experience to pull it off for a more formal occasion. If you get it right, this dish is divine.

$^1/_2$pt (300ml) nage (see recipe below)
6fl oz (165ml) nage butter sauce (see recipe below)
12 pieces of cooked fresh or dried pasta approx. $2^1/_2$in. (6cm) square
$1^1/_2$lb (675g) mussels
6oz (175g) spinach leaves
1 tbsp chopped fresh herbs – tarragon, coriander, chervil, parsley
2 large ripe plum or stem tomatoes
half a glass of white wine
pinch of saffron stamens
18oz (500g) skinned and boned monkfish tail
2 tbsp sunflower oil
Maldon salt
fresh-ground pepper
lemon juice

1. Make nage and use this to make nage butter sauce (see recipe below).
2. If making fresh pasta (see page 85), do so in advance.
3. Wash and de-beard mussels. Wash and pick over spinach leaves, taking out stalks and discarding yellow bits. Chop fresh herbs. Skin, de-seed and dice the tomatoes.
4. Heat a large pan until it is very hot and add the cleaned and drained mussels.
5. Splash in the wine and quickly whack on a tight-fitting lid.
6. Steam the mussels until all are opened – approx. 2–3 minutes. Drain, reserve jus and pick the mussels from the shells.
7. Warm sauce, add saffron and allow to infuse.
8. In a hot frying-pan sear the monkfish tails using the sunflower oil until browned all over. Season with Maldon salt, fresh-ground white pepper and

lemon juice.

9. Place the pan with the tails in it in a warm place and allow the fish to relax for 5–15 minutes.
10. Warm the pasta sheets through in the mussel jus.
11. Quickly stir-fry the spinach in the olive oil until the leaves are just wilted – approx. 1–2 minutes. Season with salt, pepper and lemon juice.
12. Add the mussels and the diced tomato to the nage butter sauce and heat through. Add the chopped herbs and check seasoning.
13. Slice the monkfish into 16 thin pieces.

Nage
1 large onion
1 leek, well trimmed
2 sticks celery
1 bulb fennel (optional)
4 large peeled carrots
1 head garlic – sliced in half across its equator
8 crushed white peppercorns
1 tsp pink peppercorns
1 star anise
1 bay leaf
1^1/$_2$oz (40g) mixed fresh herbs
^{1}/$_2$pt (300ml) white wine

1. Dice all the vegetables into ^{3}/$_4$in. (2cm) dice and place in a pot and cover with water.
2. Bring to the boil and simmer for 8 minutes, then add the herbs and simmer for a further 3 minutes.
3. Add the white wine and remove from heat, then cool and allow to marinade for 48 hours.
4. When marinaded strain stock through a fine sieve and use at once or freeze.

Nage butter sauce
MAKES ^{1}/$_4$PT (150ML)
^{1}/$_2$pt (300ml) nage (see above)
3^1/$_2$oz (90g) cold diced butter
salt and pepper
lemon juice

1. Place nage in a deep, straight-sided saucepan, bring to the boil and reduce by 80 per cent.

2. Remove from heat and add butter, working it in with a hand blender until all of the butter is melted and incorporated. It may be necessary to return the pan to the stove for a short period, thus raising the temperature of the mixture to prevent it from beginning to solidify and split. When fully incorporated, the mix should be a pale yellow colour without any trace of solids. Season with salt, pepper and lemon juice.

NOTE

The sauce needs to be kept warm before using. If it is allowed to cool and you attempt to reheat it, it will split. Should this happen, the sauce can be rescued by boiling a little double cream in the bottom of a pan and then slowly pouring it on the hot split sauce and working it in with the hand blender.

To serve the dish

Place a sheet of hot pasta on a plate or, preferably, in a shallow bowl. Place a little spinach on top, then a piece of monkfish, then a spoonful of mussel-and-tomato sauce. Repeat three times, then do the same with the other three bowls. Then divide out the remaining sauce. Some nice bread is a good way of mopping up the juices.

Fillet of cod with mashed potato and spring onion and a caviar-butter sauce

SERVES 4

This dish is really posh fish pie, but the large flakes of cod, the creamy mash and the buttery sauce combine to provide an almost sensual eating experience. Secrets of success: do not overcook the cod and make sure the potatoes are thoroughly cooked and then dried before mashing. If you don't feel like using the caviar (and it is an extravagance), then double the amount of chives in the sauce.

$^1/_2$pt (300ml) nage
2 x No. 40 baking potatoes, preferably Maris Piper, about 1$^1/_2$lb (675g) in
    weight, peeled and quartered
2oz (50g) melted butter
1fl oz (25ml) olive oil
4 finely sliced spring onions
$^1/_4$pt (150ml) nage butter sauce (see recipe below)
Maldon salt
ground white pepper
4 x 5oz (150g) boneless cod fillets
2 tsp nage or white wine
lemon juice
6oz (175g) spinach leaves
1 tsp Sevruga caviar (optional)
2 tsp chopped chives (or 4tsp if not using caviar)

1. Make $^1/_2$pt nage (see recipe on page 88).
2. Carefully boil/simmer the potatoes in salted water until just tender – approx. 20–30 minutes. Drain and dry out in a low-heat oven for 10 minutes.
3. Take out the dried potatoes and mash them using a masher or pass through a mouli into a bowl. Add the melted butter, olive oil, spring onions and season.
4. Beat this mixture well together with a wooden spoon and place in a dish, cover with foil and place in the oven on a low heat.
5. Make a nage butter sauce (see recipe below).
6. Season the nage butter sauce with Maldon salt, pepper and lemon juice.
7. Preheat oven to 400°F/200°C/Gas Mark 6 and on the stove start to heat a pan for the spinach.
8. Place the cod fillets on a well-buttered baking dish, season and pour in 2 tbsp

of nage or white wine. Dot the top of the cod with butter and squeeze a little lemon juice over it.

9. Cook the cod in the preheated oven for only 4–5 minutes. The cod should be just cooked, still translucent and not cracked.

10. While the cod is cooking, quickly stir-fry the spinach in olive oil and season.

11. Remove warmed nage butter sauce from heat and add caviar and seasoning. Add the chives at the last minute.

Nage butter sauce
MAKES $^1/_4$PT (150ML)
$^1/_2$pt (300ml) nage (see page 88)
$3^1/_2$oz (90g) cold diced butter
salt and pepper
lemon juice

1. Place nage in a deep, straight-sided saucepan, bring to the boil and reduce by 80 per cent.

2. Remove from heat and add butter, working it in with a hand blender until all of the butter is melted and incorporated. It may be necessary to return the pan to the stove for a short period, thus raising the temperature of the mixture to prevent it from beginning to solidify and split. When fully incorporated, the mix should be a pale yellow colour without any trace of solids. Season with salt, pepper and lemon juice.

NOTE
The sauce needs to be kept warm before using. If it is allowed to cool and you attempt to reheat it, it will split. Should this happen, the sauce can be rescued by boiling a little double cream in the bottom of a pan and then slowly pouring it on the hot split sauce and working it in with the hand blender.

To serve the dish
Place a little spinach on the bottom of a plate or shallow bowl. Place a scoop of potato on top of the spinach. Flatten the potato slighltly and place cod on top. Spoon caviar butter sauce over the cod.

Noisettes of roe deer, stir-fried cabbage with garlic and juniper and a bitter-chocolate sauce served with rosti potatoes

SERVES 6

To ensure the success of a more complicated dish like this, you must plan ahead. Make sure you have the stocks in your freezer. Order the venison from a good game dealer. Make the sauce at least a day in advance (it, too, could be frozen before the addition of the butter and the chocolate). Make the rosti potatoes during the day and reheat them in a slow oven. Doing all this in advance leaves just the cooking of the meat and the cabbage to the last minute.

saddle of roe deer – order from a game dealer and ask for it to be prepared in the same way as lamb, loin removed and trimmed, bones chopped and trimmings reserved
4oz (100g) butter
$^1/_2$ onion, finely sliced
$1^1/_2$ crushed cloves garlic
sprig thyme
1 bay leaf
5 crushed juniper berries
5 crushed white peppercorns
2oz (50g) sliced button mushrooms
10fl oz (300ml) red wine
8fl oz (250ml) chicken stock (see recipe below)
8fl oz (250ml) beef stock (see recipe below)
rosti potatoes (see recipe below)
1 finely shredded savoy cabbage
1oz (25g) duck fat or sunflower oil
$^1/_4$oz (6g) bitter chocolate
seasoning

1. The sauce is best done the day before. Roast the bones. Brown the trimmings in 3oz (75g) butter with the bones, onion, 1 clove of garlic, thyme, bay leaf, 1 crushed juniper berry, peppercorns and mushrooms until all have a good colour.
2. Deglaze the mixture with the wine and reduce until all of the liquid has gone.
3. Add the stocks and simmer until thickened – approx. 40 minutes.

4. Strain the mixture through a chinois and leave to settle, then skim the fat from the top and put to one side.

5. Make the rosti potatoes in advance.

6. On the day of the meal, stir-fry the shredded cabbage, garlic and 4 crushed juniper berries in the fat or oil until softened – approx. 4 minutes. Season and keep warm.

7. Now cut the venison loins into $1^1/_2$oz (40g) pieces and form into noisettes by gently knocking them flat on the open grain end. Season well.

8. Brown the venison noisettes on each side in an ounce of butter and 1 tbsp sunflower oil. Leave in the pan on a warm shelf – this should be all the cooking they need. They can be kept in this state for up to 15 minutes.

9. Just before serving, pop the noisettes back into the oven for 90 seconds.

10. Add the chocolate to the sauce just before serving and check the seasoning on the sauce.

Chicken stock

carcases of 3 chickens with skins and fat removed, and washed and drained
1 large carrot, quartered
2 med. leeks and 2 sticks of celery all halved lengthwise
1 onion with skin on quartered
1 small bulb garlic halved
6 white peppercorns
1 bay leaf
1 sprig thyme
$^1/_2$oz (15g) parsley or tarragon stalks

1. Place carcases into a large pot (large enough so that the bones only take up half of the depth of pot), cover them completely with cold water and bring to the boil.

2. Once boiling hard, skim off all of the scum and fat from the surface using a skimmer. Reduce the heat and simmer for 3 hours.

3. Remove from heat and empty contents into a colander set over a bowl.

4. Pass the stock through a chinois into a tall polypropylene container or pint jug and allow to cool by placing container into a sink of cold water.

5. When cool, place in fridge overnight until fat settles on top. Skim off fat and spoon out jellied stock into tube and freeze immediately.

NOTE
1. In summer it is best to freeze stock immediately, while in winter it will keep for up to 48 hours in the fridge.
2. Good fish and chicken stock should form a slight jelly consistency.
3. Always make stock in advance and freeze, making as large a quantity as possible at a time.
4. Always cut whole garlic heads across their 'equators'.

Beef stock
MAKES 4–5PT (2^1/$_2$–3L) (BUT CAN BE FROZEN)
10lb (4^1/$_2$kg) beef knuckle
1 pig's trotter
1lb (450g) shin
3 tbsp marrow fat
2 large carrots
2 large onions
2 large leeks
3 sticks of celery
1 head of garlic
^{1}/$_2$oz (12g) mixed parsley and tarragon stalks
3 plum tomatoes
2 tbsp tomato purée
^{1}/$_2$pt (300ml) red wine
1 bay leaf
1 sprig of thyme
12 black peppercorns

1. Cut the vegetables into large dice. Cut the head of garlic in half. Quarter the plum tomatoes.
2. Roast the bones in the oven at 200°C/400°F/Gas Mark 6 for 1 hour.
3. Reserve the marrow fat from the roasted bones.
4. Put 3 tbsp of the marrow fat into a pan and add the diced carrots, leeks, celery and onions and cook until brown. Stir while cooking.
5. Add the parsley, tarragon, bay leaf, thyme, garlic and peppercorns.
6. Add the tomato purée and quartered plum tomatoes and cook for two minutes.
7. Add the red wine and reduce the mixture right down.
8. Add the bones, the trotter, the shin of beef and enough cold water to cover the bones.
9. Bring to the boil, skimming all the time.
10. Turn down the heat and simmer for at least 8 hours (preferably

overnight).

11. Remove from pan. Pass the liquid and cool. Skim off fat.
12. Put in a stock pot and reduce by half, skimming all the time.
13. Leave to cool. This recipe will provide you with 4–5pt ($2^1/_2$–3l) stock. The unused stock can be frozen for up to 2 months.

Rosti potatoes

1lb (450g) peeled Golden Wonder or Cyprus potatoes
3oz (75g) melted clarified butter
salt and freshly ground white pepper

1. Grate the potatoes using either a mandolin or box grater on to a clean tea towel. Wring out all of the excess moisture from the grated potatoes by twisting them in a tight ball shape with the towel. Place the dried potato in a bowl and add some melted clarified butter and seasoning. Then do one of the following:

2a. Heat 4 tbsps of clarified butter in 4 blini pans and divide the potatoes between the pans, pushing down to ensure that the potato is evenly covering the pan. Cook until you see traces of colour at the edge, then turn over and complete cooking until the rostis are golden coloured on both sides. Drain on a wire rack. The rostis may be made up to 6 hours in advance and left at room temperature until you are ready to use them. They can be reheated in a medium oven.

2b. As above, but cook the rosti in a large pan and use a pastry cutter to shape and make individual rostis.

2c. Cook one large rosti, and when ready cut into 4 quarters.

To serve the dish

Place a bed of cabbage in the centre of the plate. Place a warm potato rosti on top of the cabbage. Arrange the three noisettes on top. Pour the sauce over the venison.

Escalope of salmon with a compote of avocado and tomato in a basil-butter sauce

SERVES 4

This has become one of my signature dishes. It is relatively easy to make once you have mastered the nage butter sauce. The secret is not to overcook the salmon. All the other ingredients can be made in advance, leaving you free to concentrate on the dish at the last moment. Ensure that the frying-pan is very hot and don't try to move the fish until you see a brown edge appear on the fillet.

4 x 3oz (75g) thin $^{3}/_{8}$in. (4mm) escalopes of salmon
18fl oz (550ml) of nage (see recipe below)
5oz (150g) unsalted butter
seasoning
avocado compote (see recipe below)
fresh-ground white pepper
peanut or sunflower oil
lemon juice
18 leaves freshly picked basil

1. Make sure the fish is cut on the diagonal. (Any good fish merchant should be able to do this for you.)
2. Reduce the nage by three-quarters to 4fl oz (100ml) by rapid boiling on the stove.
3. Dice the unsalted butter and whisk it into the nage using a wand/stick liquidiser (or similar). Season the mixture. Keep warm at the side – if it goes cold, it will set and split.
4. Now make the avocado compote (see recipe below).
5. Now take your salmon escalopes and quickly fry in peanut or sunflower oil in a hot pan on the best side of the salmon only for approx. 2 minutes until crisp. When ready, the fish should have a seared appearance, dark at the edges.
6. Remove from the pan and place uncooked-side down. Squeeze lemon juice over the salmon and season with Maldon salt and the fresh-ground white pepper.
7. Now return to your nage and add the chopped basil at the last minute.

Nage
1 large onion
1 leek, well trimmed
2 sticks celery
1 bulb fennel (optional)
4 large peeled carrots
1 head garlic – sliced in half across its equator
8 crushed white peppercorns
1 tsp pink peppercorns
1 star anise
1 bay leaf
$1^1/_2$oz (40g) mixed fresh herbs
$^1/_2$pt (300ml) white wine

1. Dice all the vegetables into $^3/_4$in. (2cm) dice and place in a pot and cover with water.
2. Bring to the boil and simmer for 8 minutes, then add the herbs and simmer for a further 3 minutes.
3. Add the white wine and remove from heat, then cool and allow to marinade for 48 hours.
4. When marinaded strain stock through a fine sieve and use at once or freeze.

Avocado compote
1 large, ripe avocado, preferably with crinkly skin
2 ripe plum tomatoes
1 tbsp extra-virgin olive oil
juice of a lime
dash of Worcester sauce
dash of Tabasco
4 leaves finely chopped basil
Maldon salt
fresh-ground white pepper

1. Skin avocado and chop into smallish dish.
2. Skin and quarter the tomatoes, removing the seeds. Chop into concasse.
3. Mix avocado and tomato.
4. Add the olive oil to the mixture along with lime juice, Worcester sauce, Tabasco sauce, basil and seasoning.

To serve the dish

Place a dollop of compote in the centre of the plate. Pour nage sauce over and around the compote. Place the escalope on top.

Strawberry pavlova with raspberry sauce

SERVES 6

This is easy-peasy to do. The pavlova bases can be made up to seven days ahead, and the cream added up to 12 hours ahead. Instead of strawberries and raspberries, you can try brambles, nectarines, pineapple or even kiwifruit.

5oz egg whites
8oz (225g) caster sugar
1 tbsp lemon juice and 1 tsp cornflour slaked together
12oz (350g) raspberries
1oz (25g) icing sugar
1 tbsp lemon juice on its own
15fl oz (450ml) double cream
12oz (350g) strawberries

1. The pavlova can be made well in advance. Whisk the egg whites in a mixer until they start to thicken, and add the sugar a little at a time until fully incorporated. The point at which you start adding the sugar is all-important – too soon and the meringue will not bulk up enough; too late and it splits.
2. When all the sugar has been added, pour on the lemon juice and cornflour.
3. Whisk on full speed for approx. 6–8 minutes and the meringue should be nice and thick and shiny.
4. Line a shallow baking tin (6in. x 4in. x 1in./15 cm x 10 cm x 2$^{1}/_{2}$cm) with a little oil and grease-proof paper. Spoon the meringue into the tin and smooth down with a palette knife.
5. Bake in a warm oven at 310°F/160°C/Gas Mark 2$^{1}/_{2}$ for 45 minutes until slightly risen and lightly browned on top.
6. Make the raspberry sauce by placing the raspberries, icing sugar and 1 tbsp lemon juice in a blender and whizz for 45 seconds. Pass the mixture through a fine sieve into a bowl and refrigerate.
7. When the meringue is baked, remove from oven, allow to cool and cover with cling film – this base will keep for up to 7 days at room temperature.
8. Turn the cooled-down pavlova out on to a tray – same size if possible.
9. Whisk the 15fl oz (450ml) double cream on its own until it reaches a soft peak – do not overwork the cream.
10. Using a spatula, spread the cream over the pavlova and smooth to form a clean shape with a flat top.

11. Using a thin, sharp knife, divide the pavlova into 12 equal squares.
12. Thinly slice the strawberries.
13. Lift out each square and decorate each individually with thinly sliced strawberries.
14. Place the decorated pavlova on a plate and pour round with the raspberry sauce.

Armagnac parfait with prunes and Earl Grey syrup

SERVES 8

*The ultimate standby dessert and probably the most popular dessert at Braeval
Old Mill. This simple, elegant dish continues to give me pleasure, having been on
our menu for the last four years. The cleverness in the parfait is that the Armagnac
not only flavours the parfait but also acts as an anti-freeze, allowing you to serve it
straight from the freezer – unlike normal ice-cream, which has to be given time to
soften first. The parfait keeps for up to 14 days in the freezer. The prunes, once
marinated, just seem to keep improving. We've kept them for as long as three
months and the flavour was wonderful. This dish is unusual in that the syrup is
made two weeks before and the parfait 12 hours prior, leaving very little that
needs to be done on the night. I love the contrast of the hot and cold in desserts,
and this is a perfect example.*

1pt (600ml) sugar syrup – equal parts sugar and water
1tbsp Earl Grey tea leaves
32 Agen prunes, stoned
lemon juice
3fl oz (75ml) good Armagnac
5 egg yolks
3oz (75g) sugar dissolved in a little water
$^1\!/_2$pt (300ml) double cream

1. Prepare the syrup 2 weeks before. Bring a pint of sugar syrup to the boil. Add
   the tea leaves and allow to infuse for 6 minutes.
2. Pass the syrup through a chinois and add the prunes to the still-hot syrup.
   Season with lemon juice and about 1fl oz (25ml) of the Armagnac.
3. Place in a tub and store in the fridge.
4. Prepare the parfait at least 12 hours before. In a food mixer, whisk the egg
   yolks until very pale and well-risen in volume. Whip the cream with 2fl oz
   (50ml) of Armagnac until ribbony.
5. Boil the 3oz (75g) sugar until it reaches the 'softball' stage.
6. With the mixer running on full speed, slowly pour the syrup on to the yolks.
   When fully incorporated, reduce the speed to half and whisk for a further 4–5
   minutes.
7. Fold the yolk mix and whipped cream together and pour into Dariole moulds
   – freeze immediately.

8. Prior to the meal, heat 4 prunes per person in a little syrup.
9. To serve the parfait, run the tip of a knife around the top of the parfait mould, invert and tap on a hard surface to release the contents.

To serve the dish

Place the parfait in the centre of the plate. Arrange 4 prunes around. Drizzle a little syrup over the prunes.

CHAPTER SIX

JIM GRAHAM

I BECAME interested in mushrooms about ten years ago when I was walking with my children in the woods just up from Cupar, where I live. We came across a woodcutter's cottage. It wasn't long empty, as the woodcutter had only recently fallen victim to recession. And it was there beside the woodcutter's cottage that I picked my first mushrooms. It was a chanterelle. Unfortunately, it was what's known as a false chanterelle. Luckily, I had taken it to an elderly couple who knew about such things and made sure I didn't eat it. And after that, anything I picked I brought to them for identification. I was amazed to find such an abundance of mushrooms literally on my doorstep.

I pick chanterelles from spring to early summer, ceps from early summer to the first frost, and about four years ago I started picking St George's, which are very tasty and excellent in soups. I've also recently found ceps growing in pine-woods rather than the more usual beech-woods.

These days I can get through 15–20lb a week of freshly picked mushrooms in season. To keep me going through the winter, I make mushroom ketchup from field and cultivated mushrooms. This can be quite intense, and also salty, and I use it sparingly. I've also tried preserving mushrooms in olive oil, but this required boiling the mushrooms lightly in a brine, which produced a loss of flavour. Now I'm preserving the mushrooms in duck fat, which allows the mushrooms to keep their flavour. The most common way to preserve mushrooms, which I also do, is to dry them. Dried mushrooms keep their flavour well, but the only drawback is that this method requires really a lot of mushrooms. If I'd had to buy all the mushrooms, I doubt if I would have used them so much or experimented with them as much. Mushrooms are very versatile. They're very quick to cook – usually give them a quick stir fry.

The mushroom dish I've included here – *panfried terrine of wild mushroom, goat's cheese and potato served with mixed salad leaves in a herb vinaigrette* – is an adaptation of another recipe. The original impulse came from a recipe by the great French chef Georges Blanc. I'd been developing a recipe for a terrine of mushroom, aubergine and red pepper which I serve in the restaurant with an orange-scented vinaigrette. From that I thought of a terrine combining goat's cheese and potato, and then I had the idea of incorporating ricotta cheese along with the mushrooms. I get some of my best ideas when I'm working in the vegetable garden. I grow herbs and vegetables for the restaurant. I grow six different types of lettuce, courgettes, turnips, leeks and orange beetroot, which, unlike red beetroot, does not bleed on the plate. I grow camomile, which we use for herb teas. I like growing food – it gives me a sense of what's possible. When I'm gardening I relax, and that's when the ideas for dishes come.

The idea for *smoked haddock in a cream-leek sauce on a bed of mashed potato* came to me when I was in the garden. It's a very good starter, and I serve it as a canapé. I was looking for something distinctive to serve as a canapé. I'd done a quiche and I'd done a chicken liver and parma ham on toast, but I felt none of these were enough of a signature dish. Down the road at St Monans they make smoked haddock the natural way. I was thinking of smoked haddock, and mashed potato seemed a natural accompaniment. The leek sauce adds a complementary flavour. It's very simple, but very more-ish.

I cook a lot of fish – we are so well served for fresh fish in Fife. It's quite an unusual recipe for adding flavour to blander fish. It's actually an adaptation of the piccatta batter that is more usually found on light-coloured meats such as veal and pork. The recipe is very quick and simple, and ideal for use on many kinds of fish.

My wife, Amanda, does our desserts. Her *layered hazelnut meringue discs filled with mascarpone cheese and apricots on an apricot coulis* started out as an apricot and ordinary meringue dish, based on an idea that she had developed from her mother. People like meringue but usually as a cake rather than as a dessert. We had been serving poached apricots and meringue, and Amanda developed the idea of making the meringues in discs and serving them in layers. Then she had the idea of making the meringues hazelnut-flavour to give the dish an extra dimension. Then the cheese was added. Mascarpone is a soft cheese and quite sweet, more a cream really than a cheese. The meringue discs are harder to make than ordinary meringue, but it's still a very simple dish, more like putting simple components together to create a special effect.

I knew what I wanted to be when I was 12. I was either going to be a baker or a chef. My father had been a blacksmith and later ran a hotel but he was a good cook, a great maker of soups, and even back in the 1960s he was serving the kind of salads that we take for granted today. My mother was a very good baker. However, there was no opening as a baker in Pitlochry where we lived so I went to work for a chef of the old school.

I had been working for 13 years in a variety of restaurants and hotels before I took the plunge and opened Ostlers Close in 1981. I have a tiny kitchen with one solid-top stove and a six-ring burner. I work almost entirely on my own, and since the restaurant itself is so small, seating only 26, I often have the feeling that I'm cooking at home.

JIM GRAHAM runs Ostlers Close in Cupar, Fife, with his wife, Amanda. In 1989 the restaurant was awarded the Taste of Scotland Prestige Award and in 1991 was named *Scottish Field* Restaurant of the Year. From 1994 it received 3 AA rosettes for cuisine, joining a handful of Scottish restaurants ranked in that category.

Panfried terrine of wild mushroom, goat's cheese and potato served with mixed salad leaves in a herb vinaigrette

SERVES 4 OR MORE

This recipe is ideal for a vegetarian starter or main course. And it has the added advantage that it can be made in advance and kept in the refrigerator for a few days.

2lb (900g) potatoes
$^1/_4$pt (150ml) olive oil
6oz (175g) clarified butter
4oz (100–125g) wild mushrooms or flat cultivated, depending on time of year
8oz (225g) firm goat's cheese (e.g. Bonnet)
2oz (50g) ricotta cheese
4oz (100g) mixed salad leaves, especially rocket if possible
herb vinaigrette (see recipe below)

1. Peel potatoes and shape into $^1/_5$in. ($^1/_2$cm)-thick rectangles.
2. Fry potato slices in a mix of olive oil and clarified butter. Do not brown – leave a bite.
3. Grease and line a 12in. (30cm) Le Creuset mould with cling film.
4. Line the base and sides with two layers of potato.
5. Sauté the mushrooms in the leftover butter/oil mixture.
6. Dice the goat's cheese and mix in food processor to rough-crumb stage. Stir in the ricotta.
7. Put a layer of cheese mix on top of the potato layer, then add mushrooms, then two layers of potato. Repeat this process until you have reached the top of the terrine. Fold over the excess potato flaps.
8. Seal with cling film and weigh down for at least 24 hours in the fridge.
9. Slice the terrine and fry on one side in olive oil.
10. Finish heating the slices in oven at 400°F/200°C/Gas Mark 6 for 5 minutes.

Herb vinaigrette

3fl oz (75ml) virgin olive oil
1^1/$_2$fl oz (40ml) balsamic vinegar
1fl oz (25ml) hazelnut oil
juice of half a lemon
1^1/$_2$tsp honey
seasoning
2oz (50g) chopped fresh herbs – parsley, chervil, basil, chives

Toss ingredients together in a bowl.

To serve the dish

Arrange the terrine on the plate. Serve with the mixed salad leaves and the herb vinaigrette.

Confit of farmed duck leg with preserved wild mushrooms in a balsamic-vinegar-and-nut-oil dressing

SERVES 4

This is a favourite dish of many of our customers, who say that it is better than the confit they have eaten in France. If this is true, part of the reason lies with the quality of the free-range ducks which are supplied to us by a local lady, who is a real gem. The actual cooking time on the day of eating the dish is minimal – all the work is done well in advance.

4 duck leg joints
2 tbsp sea-salt
1lb (450g) duck fat or cooking lard
bay leaf
sprig of thyme
1oz (25g) dried cep or 4oz (100–125g) cep preserved in duck fat or 4oz
    ordinary mushrooms such as oyster or shiitaki
balasamic vinaigrette with nut oil (see recipe below)

1. Trim duck legs from the sinew and cut off end knuckle bone.
2. Place the duck legs in a non-metallic container and sprinkle with sea-salt, bay leaf and thyme.
3. Cover the container and place in the fridge for 24 hours.
4. After 24 hours, remove the container from the fridge and wash off the salt.
5. Place in a high-sided roasting tin with the additional fat and cook in a slow oven at 275°F/140°C/Gas Mark 1 (if you have an Aga, cook in the bottom oven) for about 8 hours. After cooking, the meat should be tender and almost ready to fall from the bone.
6. Lift out the duck legs gently into a non-metallic container.
7. Slowly pour the fat juices from the duck into a bowl. Allow this to separate and cool before pouring the fat only over the duck legs. Make sure they are completely covered, then cover with grease-proof paper.
8. Cool completely, then refrigerate. These can stay in the fridge for 1–2 months if completely sealed. We often use them after 1 week, once the flavour has matured. The juices can also be refrigerated to add to the sauce.
9. When you are ready to eat the dish, simply remove the duck legs from the fat and put into a hot frying-pan to crispen.

10. Then put the duck legs into a hot oven at 400°F/200°C/Gas Mark 6 to heat through completely.
11. Dry with absorbent paper before serving.
12. Make up vinaigrette (see recipe below), warm it gently and add 3 tbsp of duck juices.
13. With a little of the duck fat, cook the preserved mushrooms.

Balsamic vinaigrette with nut oil
3fl oz (75ml) virgin olive oil
1^1/$_2$fl oz (50ml) balsamic vinaigrette
1fl oz (25ml) hazelnut oil
juice of half a lemon
1^1/$_2$tsp honey

Mix the ingredients together in a bowl.

To serve the dish
Make a bed of mushrooms on the plate, lay the duck legs on top and coat the plate with the sauce.

East Neuk bouillabaisse

SERVES 6

This is a variation on the traditional Mediterranean fish soup, using a variety of local seafood and other local ingredients.

2 large onions
2 celery sticks
1 leek
1 carrot
5 tomatoes
6 pieces of French stick
1 tbsp olive oil
3 cloves garlic crushed with salt
sprig of thyme
sprig of parsley
sprig of fennel
pinch of curry powder
1 piece dried orange peel
3pt (1.8l) fish stock or water
few strands of saffron
$^{1}/_{4}$pt (150ml) olive oil
2lb (900g) mixed fish pieces, e.g. mackerel, salmon, haddock, whiting,
    langoustine, sole, monkfish, turbot

1. Chop the onions and the celery. Dice the leek and carrot. Skin and de-seed the tomatoes. Cut up the French bread and put into the oven to toast.
2. Put 1 tbsp of olive oil in a soup pan, add the vegetables and sweat them off.
3. Add garlic, herbs, tomatoes, tomato purée and orange peel.
4. Add the stock, saffron and the rest of the olive oil and bring to the boil. Simmer for about 15 minutes. Check for seasoning.
5. Cut the fish pieces up into a uniform size. Keep the various types separate.
6. Ten minutes before serving, add the fish to the simmering soup using the firmer-textured fish first. Be careful not to boil or overcook at this stage.

To serve the dish
Place pieces of the dried French stick into large soup bowls. Pour the soup on to the bread. Garnish with chopped chives/parsley.

Smoked haddock in a cream-leek sauce on a bed of mashed potato

SERVES 4

This recipe was originally devised as a canapé before dinner. But it was so popular that sometimes we now serve it as a starter on our lunch menu. In many ways, it is an ideal starter because it is simple to make and the strength of the flavour always takes people by surprise.

1lb (450g) potatoes
3oz (75g) butter
1/4pt (150ml) cream and 1 tbsp extra (optional)
1 medium leek
1lb (440g) undyed smoked haddock fillets
1/4pt (150ml) fish stock

1. Peel the potatoes and boil in salted water until cooked. Drain, dry and mash with 1oz (25g) butter, adding 1 tbsp of cream if the mash is still very tight. To obtain a smoother purée you can pass it through a mouli or a sieve.
2. Cut off a quarter of the leek and chop finely. Sweat this off in 1oz (25g) butter.
3. Add whole haddock fillets and stock. Poach gently until just cooked and no more.
4. Remove fish from juices and keep warm.
5. Add the rest of the cream to the sauce. Reduce by half. Check for seasoning. Whisk in the butter.
6. Use the remainder of the leek as a fine julienne. Deep fry the julienne of leek in hot sunflower oil until light golden. (The julienne is optional.)

To serve the dish
Place equal portions of mashed potato on four warm plates. Shape the potato into a neat, round shape. With the back of a spoon, make a well in the middle of the potato. Place flaked fish fillets on top of the potato. Sieve sauce around the sides of the plate. Garnish with the deep-fried julienne of leek.

Roast breast of wood pigeon on a bed of lentil du Puy and wild mushrooms in a red-wine sauce

SERVES 4

Pigeon is a very underestimated dish. If properly prepared, it can be quite delicious. And because the bird is small, it is easier to control the cooking. The size of the bird also helps in serving the portions. This is another dish that we serve as a starter.

8oz (225g) lentil du Puy
4 pigeons
red-wine sauce (see recipe below)
8 shallots
1pt (600ml) chicken stock
1 bay leaf
6oz (175g) fresh wild mushrooms or 1oz (25g) dried mushrooms
2oz (50g) butter
sunflower oil or olive oil – enough to coat the pan

1. Soak lentil du Puy in cold water overnight. Drain the next day.
2. Ready (or ask your butcher to do it) the pigeons by removing the breasts and holding the carcase for sauce.
3. Make the red-wine sauce (see recipe below), which has to simmer for 2 hours.
4. Finely chop the shallots.
5. Sweat off half the shallots in the oil, add the drained lentils and mix in with the oil. Add the chicken stock and the bay leaf. Season. Bring to the boil and simmer until cooked.
6. Chop the fresh mushrooms (or soak the dried ones and then chop them). Melt butter in a separate pan from the lentils. Add the remaining shallots, then add the mushrooms.
7. Cook the mushrooms and add the lentils to this mix. Keep warm.
8. Season the pigeon breasts and then seal the meat in hot pan with olive oil.
9. Roast the pigeon breasts in a hot oven at 400°F/200°C/Gas Mark 6 for about 5 minutes. The meat should still be springy to the touch. Then rest the pigeon breasts and keep warm for 5 minutes before carving.

Jim Graham

PANFRIED TERRINE OF WILD MUSHROOM, GOAT'S CHEESE AND POTATO SERVED WITH MIXED
SALAD LEAVES IN A HERB VINAIGRETTE

FRANCES ATKINS

NICK NAIRN

DAVID WILSON AND JIM GRAHAM

Red-wine sauce

1lb (450g) mix of carrot, celery, onion and fennel
pigeon bones
1 small pig's trotter
8oz (225g) oxtail
1 clove of garlic
1 tsp coriander seed and black peppercorns
1 bay leaf
2 tbsp tomato purée
2pt (1.2l) chicken stock
1pt (600ml) red wine
1 tbsp redcurrant jelly
1 tbsp mushroom ketchup (optional)
1oz (25g) cold diced butter

1. Finely chop the carrot, celery, onion and fennel and mix together.
2. Brown the pigeon bones, pig's trotter and oxtail.
3. Add the finely chopped vegetables, garlic, spices and tomato purée.
4. Cook on a medium heat for 10 minutes until brown.
5. Add stock, red wine and redcurrant jelly. Bring to the boil, skim off the scum, and simmer for 2 hours.
6. When the simmering is complete, strain the stock, reduce to the consistency of a sauce (about $^1/_2$pt–300ml), add the mushroom ketchup. Check for seasoning. Whisk in cold diced butter.

To serve the dish

Place the mix of mushrooms and lentils on the plate. Top with the carved pigeon breasts. Surround with the red-wine sauce.

Roast fillet of salmon with a salt crust on a bed of spicy cabbage with a butter sauce

SERVES 4

Roasting seals the flavour in. It is quick and easy.

8oz (225g) savoy cabbage
olive oil
1oz (25g) mixed crushed spices – cumin, coriander, mustard seed
finely grated zest and juice of 1 lemon
$^1/_4$ crushed garlic clove
4 x 6oz (175g) salmon fillets with skin on
2 tbsp sea-salt
butter sauce (see recipe below)

1. Shred the cabbage. Blanch it and refresh it.
2. Stir-fry in a frying-pan with a little olive oil the cabbage, spices, lemon juice and rind and garlic for 2 minutes to infuse without overcooking. Set aside.
3. Take the salmon and coat the skin-side with olive oil, then dip into the salt.
4. Place salmon skin-side down in a hot frying-pan with a little oil and sear.
5. Put the frying-pan into the oven to bake for 8–10 minutes at 400°F/200°C/Gas Mark 6, until salmon flesh is cooked but moist.

Butter sauce
1pt (600ml) fish stock
$^1/_4$pt (150ml) dry vermouth
$^1/_2$pt (300ml) double cream
2oz (50g) cold diced butter
a squeeze of lemon

1. Reduce fish stock and vermouth by half.
2. Add the cream and reduce by another third.
3. Whisk in the cold diced butter.
4. Add the squeeze of lemon. Check for seasoning. Keep warm.

To serve the dish
Place mound of stir-fried cabbage in the middle of the plate. Top the cabbage with the salmon and surround the dish with the butter sauce.

114

Layered chocolate-mousse cake on a caramel sauce

SERVES 8

The dish uses a dark-chocolate mousse and a white-chocolate mousse. The recipes for the mousses can stand alone.

sponge (see recipe below)
dark-chocolate mousse (see recipe below)
white-chocolate mousse (see recipe below)
caramel sauce (see recipe below)

1. Make sponge (see recipe below).
2. Add layer of dark-chocolate mousse (see recipe below).
3. Add layer of white-chocolate mousse (see recipe below).
4. Make caramel sauce (see recipe below).

Sponge
2 eggs
2oz (50g) caster sugar
1¹/₂oz (40g) self-raising flour
¹/₂oz (15g) cocoa

1. To make the sponge, butter a 9in. (23cm) loose-bottomed, high-sided cake tin. Line with grease-proof paper.
2. Whisk 2 eggs and the caster sugar until thick and creamy white – you can tell it's ready when the mixture leaves a trail on the surface.
3. Gently fold in sieved flour and cocoa.
4. Empty mixture into cake tin and bake in a moderate oven – 375°F/190°C/Gas Mark 5 – for 15 minutes until springy to the touch.
5. When the sponge is baked, allow to cool and remove from tin.
6. Wash the tin, then butter it and line it with cling film, sides included. Place the cold sponge on the base.

Dark-chocolate mousse
6oz (175) dark chocolate
$^1/_2$oz (15g) butter
1tbsp brandy
$^1/_4$pt (100ml) double-cream, whipped
3 eggs, separated

1. To make the dark-chocolate mousse, melt the dark chocolate in a bowl over a pan of simmering (not boiling) water. Add the butter and let it melt. Add the brandy.
2. Remove the dark-chocolate mixture from the heat and stir in 3 egg yolks. Fold in $^1/_4$pt (100ml) whipped cream and then very gently fold in the 3 whisked egg whites.
3. Pour the dark-chocolate mixture on to the sponge, allow it to cool and put it in the fridge to set.

White-chocolate mousse
9oz (250g) white chocolate
2 leaves of gelatine
$^1/_2$pt (300ml) double cream, whipped
2 egg whites

1. Melt the white chocolate in a bowl over a pan of hot water. White chocolate needs a low, gentle heat to melt successfully – beating steadily helps to melt it.
2. Soak the gelatine in cold water, and when it has jellied pour off the water and melt gently.
3. Add the melted gelatine to the melted white chocolate.
4. Fold in $^1/_2$pt (300ml) whipped cream and two whisked egg whites.
5. Pour on top of the dark-chocolate mousse, put in fridge when cool.

Caramel sauce

5fl oz (150ml) water
5oz (150g) sugar
9fl oz (250ml) double cream
1 egg yolk

1. Caramelise the sugar and water in a heavy-bottomed pan.
2. Brush down sides of pan with water and pastry brush to prevent burning when you then add the cream.
3. Boil for 3 minutes.
4. Remove from heat and whisk in the egg yolk.
5. Allow to cool.

To serve the dish

Coat the plates with sauce. Lift the cake out of the tin using the sides of cling film. Cut the cake into eight slices with a sharp knife. After each slice, dip the knife into a container of hot water (otherwise the dark-chocolate mousse will colour the white-chocolate mousse).

Layered hazelnut meringue discs filled with mascarpone cheese and apricots on an apricot coulis

SERVES 4

This is quite an unusual dessert, partly because of the shape of the meringues, and partly due to the flavour of the hazelnut.

1oz (25g) grand hazelnuts
9oz (250g) tub mascarpone cheese
2 egg whites
4oz (100–125g) caster sugar
$^1/_4$tsp vanilla
$^1/_2$pt (300ml) stock syrup – $^1/_2$pt (300ml) water, 8oz (225g) granulated sugar
2lb (900g) apricots
1tbsp peach schnapps

1. Lightly toast the grand hazelnuts in oven or under grill and allow to cool.
2. Lightly whip the mascarpone.
3. Whisk egg whites until firm. Fold in the sugar and the cooled grand hazelnuts along with the vanilla to make the meringue mix.
4. Line a flat baking sheet with grease-proof paper. Then with the back of a spoon shape the meringue mix into circles about 5in. (12cm) in diameter and $^1/_8$in. (3mm) thick. Two discs are required for each person – the mix may produce more than you need but it's impractical to make a smaller quantity and any leftover can be stored away.
5. Bake in a slow oven for about 1 hour at 275°F/140°C/Gas Mark 1 until crisp.
6. Make your stock syrup by boiling the water and sugar to a syrup.
7. Halve and stone 1lb (450g) of the apricots and poach them lightly until just cooked. Then remove from heat and allow to cool.
8. Use the remaining apricots to make the coulis. Halve and stone these apricots. Cook them in the juices of the poached apricots until they are soft enough to purée. Sieve and add schnapps. Allow to cool.

To serve the dish
Coat the plate with the sauce. Place a meringue disc in the centre and on top put layers of apricots and mascarpone. Place the remaining meringue disc on top.

CHAPTER SEVEN

BRUCE SANGSTER

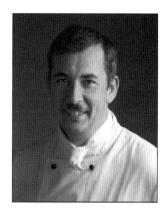

ON a trip to Singapore I observed that chefs were using deep-fried vegetables in salads. When I wondered how to apply this concept to Scottish produce, I came up with the idea of *crab gateau layered with celeriac crisps with sun-dried tomatoes*. With the sweetness of the crab, I was looking for something light. I started off with just the crisps and the crab, but I felt the dish needed something more so I added celery for texture, and coriander and ginger to give it more zing, and there's also a burst of sweet pea paw to complement the crab.

Creating dishes is spontaneous for me. My dishes usually come about because I am playing with certain ingredients. I place a strong emphasis on what food looks like, which is an unfashionable thing to do. But I can't produce dishes that lack colour – I'd rather avoid the dish than produce something that looks dull. I'm very keen on height in presentation. It's become a subconscious thing for me – most of my dishes have height, which is very pleasing to the eye. Conversely, I keep a lot of things hidden in a dish. Inside the banana parfait is pear sorbet, under slices of lamb you'll find shallots. This fits in with my notion that eating should be a discovery, carrying on the element of surprise.

BRUCE SANGSTER is the captain of the successful Scottish Culinary Olympic Team which won a record number of gold medals at the Food Asia in Singapore in 1994. Bruce began his career at the Old Course Hotel in St Andrews, Fife. He was Scottish Chef of the Year in 1989 and Egon Ronay British Lamb chef in 1990. He is currently executive chef for Lehman Brothers International in London. He is a founder member of the Scottish Chefs Association and sits on its Advisory Board.

Crab gateau layered with celeriac crisps with sun-dried tomatoes

SERVES 4

This dish was inspired after a visit to Singapore, where I observed that they were using a lot of deep-fried vegetables in salads, which add texture to some dishes.

6oz (175g) celeriac, peeled, at least 3in. (7cm) diameter
6oz (175g) freshly cooked and shelled crab meat
1 stalk celery, peeled and finely diced
2 plum tomatoes, blanched, skinned, de-seeded and diced
1 tsp fresh ginger, grated
1 small bunch coriander, finely diced
1oz (25g) sun-dried tomatoes
1 tomato, fresh and ripe
5 black olives, finely chopped
$^1/_5$oz (5g) capers
$^2/_5$ fl oz (10ml) balsamic vinegar
$^3/_5$ fl oz (15ml) olive oil
small amounts of blond frizzy, mache, baby spinach, oak leaf and radichio
2 fl oz (50ml) virgin olive oil
1 fl oz (20ml) balsamic vinegar
3oz (75g) pearls of mango, paw paw and melon
$^1/_2$oz (15g) chives, chopped

1. With a very sharp knife or mandoline, slice the celeriac into crisps, cut with a round cutter, then deep fry at 310°F/160°C/Gas Mark 2$^1/_2$ until crisp and light brown. Remove and dry on a piece of paper towel.
2. Combine the crab with the celery, tomato, ginger and coriander. Season carefully, leave in a cool place to allow the flavours to permeate with each other.
3. Stew the sun-dried tomatoes to soften the purée, mix with chopped fresh tomatoes, olives and capers. Mix in the vinegar and olive oil. Season.
4. Pick the salad leaves, lightly toss with its dressing.

To serve the dish
Layer the celeriac crisps with the crab mixture – 3 crisps and 2 layers of crab per plate. Surround with the dressed salad leaves and garnish with the mango, paw paw and melon. Finish by sprinkling with tomato dressing and chives.

Breast of maize-fed guinea-fowl on a bed of lentil du Puy with panchetta

SERVES 4

I was introduced to quality guinea-fowl by Braehead Foods about the same time as I first tasted panchetta, and along with the lentils I found that it created a nice wholesome dish for a cold winter's day.

12 shallots, peeled and split
4oz (100–125g) $^1/_4$in. (6mm) diced carrots
2oz (50g) $^1/_4$in. (6mm) diced celery
10oz (275g) lentil du Puys, washed
2oz (50g) clarified butter
1 clove garlic, crushed
2 sprigs thyme
1pt (600ml) brown chicken stock
1 bay leaf
1 pinch ground cloves
8oz (225g) peeled potatoes
$1^1/_2$oz (40g) butter
$^1/_4$pt (150ml) double cream
1 clove garlic, crushed
salt, pepper and nutmeg
4 x 7oz (200g) breasts of maize-fed guinea-fowl
4oz (100–125g) panchetta, cut into batons
$^1/_2$pt (300ml) red wine
1pt (600ml) brown chicken stock
1 sprig rubbed thyme
1oz (25g) butter
salt and pepper

1. Prepare the lentils by sweating the shallots, carrots and celery in half of the butter. Add the washed lentils, garlic, thyme and chicken stock. Bring to the boil, then add the bay leaf, thyme and clove. Cover and gently simmer for approx. 30 minutes until cooked but not overcooked. Season and reserve warm.
2. Prepare the potato by boiling in salted water until just cooked. Drain and return to the pan to steam and dry. Pass through a fine sieve to form a purée.

3. Warm the cream with the garlic and butter, then carefully beat into the potato purée. Season with salt and pepper and nutmeg. Reserve hot for use.

4. In a heavy-bottomed pan melt the other half of the butter from the lentil preparation. Having seasoned the guinea-fowl breasts, quickly brown on both sides, then remove and place on an oven-proof tray and roast at 425°F/220°C/Gas Mark 7 for 6 minutes. Remove and cover with a piece of foil to allow the meat to rest.

5. In the cooking pan fry the batons of panchetta for 2–3 minutes, remove and keep warm. In the same pan add the red wine a little at a time and quickly reduce as you do so. Then repeat with the stock until approximately a third of a pint remains. Pass this through a fine sieve or muslin into a clean pan and bring to the boil. Add the rubbed thyme and finish the sauce by mounting with the butter. Season with salt and pepper.

To serve the dish
Place the potatoes in the piping bag with a plain tube. To one side on each plate pipe a swirl to resemble a fallen-oven walnut whip. Place a small mound of lentils to the other side, then top with the guinea-fowl breasts. Add the panchetta to the sauce and spoon over and around the dish. Serve hot.

Warm lamb salad on a bed of caramelised shallots with a Dunsyre blue-cheese dressing

SERVES 4

I consider myself fortunate enough to have made it to the finals of the British Chef of the Year Competition on 4 straight occasions. In 1990 I finished third using this dish as my starter.

2 best ends of lamb, free of bone, fat and sinew
olive oil, rosemary and garlic for marinade
24 shallots, peeled and split
2 tbsp olive oil
1 tbsp caster sugar
2 fl oz (50ml) balsamic vinegar
$\frac{1}{2}$pt (300ml) brown lamb stock
4 small boquets of salad leaves – mache, frizzy, dandelion and radichio
1 fl oz (25ml) cider vinegar
3 fl oz (75ml) walnut oil
1oz (25g) celery, finely diced
$\frac{1}{2}$ clove garlic, crushed
$\frac{1}{4}$pt (150ml) dry cider
$\frac{1}{2}$pt (300ml) brown lamb stock
3 tbsp double cream
1 tbsp rosemary, finely chopped
2oz (50g) Dunsyre blue cheese, crumbled
10 cherry tomatoes, cut in half
80 small solferinos of Dunsyre blue cheese
1oz (25g) pine kernels, toasted
1 apple, cut into matchsticks
20 sprigs chervil

1. Place the loins of lamb in a shallow tray with olive oil, rosemary and garlic. Cover with cling film and leave for 4 hours, turning from time to time. Remove and drain.
2. In a thick-bottomed pan brown the shallots in a little oil. When thoroughly coloured add the sugar and caramelise. Then add the balsamic vinegar. Cook to a brown syrup, then bit by bit add the stock, reducing all the time. After approximately 15 minutes the shallots should be cooked. Reserve for use.

3. In a hot, heavy-bottomed pan sear the loins of lamb quickly, then toast for 5 minutes. Remove from the oven and allow to rest for 5–10 minutes. Meanwhile, pour off the excess fat and add the diced celery. Scrape away any sediment. Next add the garlic. After 30 seconds add the cider, reduce to a syrup then add the stock. Continue cooking until reduced to $^1/_4$pt. Add the cream and bring to the boil.

4. Mix the crisp salad leaves in a mixture of the walnut oil and vinegar and place neatly into 4 small rings.

5. Place 4 x 4in. (10 x 10cm) rings on to 4 hot plates. Place a layer of shallots into the bottom and press firmly. Carve the lamb and arrange overlapping slices on top of the shallots. Top this with salad rings.

6. Arrange 5 halves of tomato around each plate, then interspace with small pieces of the cheese balls.

7. Add the crumbled cheese to the dressing and heat through. Season with pepper and add the rosemary.

To serve the dish

Lightly nap the rings with the sauce. Sprinkle with pine nuts and apple. Decorate with chervil.

Parcel of salmon and turbot served on a chive-butter sauce with langoustine tails

SERVES 4

In 1989 I won the title of Scottish Chef of the Year with this dish. It formed the main course of that meal and still gives me great pleasure to this day.

1oz (25g) shallots
1oz (25g) parsley
1oz (25g) chives
4 plum tomatoes
4oz (100–125g) unsalted butter
4oz (100–125g) button mushrooms
4 large spring green cabbage leaves
4 x 2oz (50g) fillets of salmon
4 x 2oz (50g) fillet of turbot
$^1/_4$pt (150ml) Noilly Prat
$1^1/_2$pt (900ml) fish stock
5 fl oz (175ml) double cream
juice of half a lemon
olive oil for cooking
20 fresh tails of langoustine

1. Finely chop the shallots, parsley and chives. Blanch, skin, de-seed and dice tomato. Prepare a duxelles by cooking the shallots in 1oz (25g) of butter. Do not colour. Add the mushrooms and cook to release the liquid. Carry on cooking until dry. Add parsley and season with salt and pepper. Allow to cool.
2. Blanch the cabbage leaves and refresh in iced water. Remove the central stack and dry the leaves. Sandwich the salmon and turbot with the mushroom, then wrap in the cabbage. Seal in cling film.
3. Gently steam the parcels for 8–10 minutes, remove and rest.
4. Reduce the Noilly by half, then add the fish stock and reduce to a third of a pint. Add the cream and bring to the boil, then with a hand blender add 3oz (75g) of cold butter to thicken the sauce. Finish with the chives and lemon juice.
5. Heat olive oil in heavy-based pan, quickly fry langoustine tails. Season.
7. Heat tomato in little butter and arrange 5 tsp per plate. Top the tomato with the langoustine tails and pour the hot sauce on to the plates. To serve, remove the cling film from the parcels and cut in half.

Loin of roe deer with a barley risotto, wild mushroom and a port-wine sauce

SERVES 4

In London I find that you cannot go into a restaurant without being faced with risotto, so I felt that Scotland should have its own version.

4 x 6oz (170g) loins of roe deer, free of bone, fat and sinew
olive oil for cooking
4 Prune D'Agen, soaked in $^1/_2$pt (300ml) of port wine
1pt (600ml) home-made venison stock or veal stock
2oz (50g) unsalted butter
1oz (25g) shallots, finely chopped
1oz (25g) unsalted butter
1oz (25g) carrots and celery, finely diced
4oz (100–125g) barley, soaked and boiled in chicken stock
$^1/_4$pt (150ml) chicken stock
$^1/_4$pt (150ml) double cream
$^1/_2$oz (15g) chives, finely chopped
6oz (175g) mixed wild mushrooms – trumpet, giroles, paris browns
1oz (25g) unsalted butter
12 turned carrots, blanched
12 baby turnips, blanched
12 small asparagus tips, blanched
$^1/_4$pt (150ml) water
1oz (25g) butter
$^1/_2$ lemon
salt and pepper

1. Warm the port with the prunes, which will cause them to plump up and become soft. Remove and finely chop the prunes. Reserve for use in the final sauce.
2. For the risotto, sweat the shallots, carrots and celery in the butter, do not burn, then add the barley. Mix until well coated in butter, then, stirring continuously, add the stock a little at a time. When all the stock is added and absorbed, add the cream in the same fashion. Season and finish with chives.
3. In a hot pan seal the deer in olive oil then roast in a hot oven for 5 minutes. Remove and allow to rest in a warm place.

4. Pour off any fat and add the port wine and prune juices. Reduce by half, add the venison stock and boil rapidly. Skim and reduce to a light coating consistency. Reserve warm.
5. In another pan, sauté the cleaned wild mushrooms in butter. Season.
6. Reheat the vegetables in an emulsion of water, butter and lemon juice until nice and glazed.

To serve the dish

Place a 2in. (5cm) wide by $^{3}/_{4}$in. (2cm) deep ring on to 4 hot plates. Fill and press with the hot risotto. Cut the roe deer into 3 slices each and arrange on the plates. In between, arrange the vegetables and top the risotto with wild mushrooms. Finish the sauce by bringing to the boil and add prunes and butter. Season and pour around the plates.

Medallion of beef fillet with a brioche, bone marrow and horseradish crust on a whole grain-mustard sauce

SERVES 4

Beef is still one of the most satisfying and flavoursome dishes. This recipe provides an excellent main course.

1oz (25g) thyme, chives and parsley
2oz (50g) shallots
1/2oz (15g) tarragon
1oz (25g) fresh horseradish
4oz (100–125g) unsalted butter, cold
4oz (100–125g) brioche crumbs
3oz (75g) bone marrow, run in iced water to remove the blood
4 x 5oz (150g) medallions of Scotch beef fillet
olive oil for cooking
1 tbsp caster sugar
2 fl oz (50ml) red-wine vinegar
1/2pt (300ml) red wine – St Emillion
1pt (600ml) jellied beef stock
1 tsp whole grain Arran mustard

1. Finely chop thyme, chive, parsley and shallots. Chop tarragon. Grate horseradish. Melt 1oz (25g) of the butter and lightly fry the brioche crumbs.
2. Sweat the shallots in 1oz butter along with the mixture.
3. In a heavy-based pan seal the beef in olive oil. Brown well, then cook for 2 minutes in a hot oven. Remove, then place on a clean tray, top with the brioche crust. Dot with butter, roast for 5 minutes. Allow to rest.
4. Meanwhile, in the same pan, pour off the fat, add the sugar and caramelise, then deglaze with the vinegar. Reduce to a syrup, then little by little, add the red wine, again reducing to a syrup. Repeat with the stock until a third of a pint remains. Pass through a fine sieve then a muslin cloth into a clean pan.
5. Reboil the sauce. Add the tarragon and mustard, check seasoning and finish sauce by whisking in the cold butter.

To serve the dish
Spoon the sauce around beef and serve with vegetables.

Drambuie and raspberry mousse with crisp thistle butter biscuit

SERVES 12

In my travels during competitions I have made many friends, and I dare say a few enemies, but no greater friend and craftsman than Willie Pike, who is responsible for the creation of this dish, which was the dessert the British Team used to help win gold in the National Hot Team Kitchen held at 'Food Asia 1992'. Any mousse left over can be frozen for up to a month.

Drambuie mousse (see recipe below)
raspberry mousse (see recipe below)
raspberry glaze (see recipe below)
thistle butter biscuit (see recipe below)

1. Make the Drambuie mousse (see recipe below).
2. Make the raspberry mousse (see recipe below).
3. Make the raspberry glaze (see recipe below).
4. Make the thistle butter biscuit (see recipe below).
5. Wrap cling film around the bottom of small stainless-steel rings. Spray with a spray-release, then pour a film of the glaze into the bottom and allow to set.
6. Half-fill the moulds with the Drambuie mousse. With the aid of a piping bag, fill up the moulds by piping the raspberry mousse into the centre of the Drambuie mousse.
7. Place in the fridge to set.

Drambuie mousse
$^1/_2$pt (300ml) milk
$^1/_2$ vanilla pod, split
1 tbsp double cream
4 egg yolks
2oz (50g) caster sugar
2 egg whites
6oz (175g) sugar
water
$^1/_2$pt (300ml) lightly whipped whipping cream
$3^1/_2$ leaves gelatine
1 large measure Drambuie

129

1. To make a crème anglaise place the cream and vanilla pod in a pan and bring to the boil. Whisk the yolks and caster sugar together. Pour the milk mixture into a clean pan and slowly bring back to the heat, stirring continuously until it coats the back of a spoon. Remove the pan from the heat and sieve. Continue stirring until the mixture is cool. Be careful not to beat too vigorously or the mixture will split.

2. Make an Italienne meringue by mixing the sugar with a tiny amount of water, just enough to stop the sugar crystallising. Boil the sugar on a high heat, until large bubbles appear. Whisk up the egg whites until they are stiff peaks. Pour the boiling sugar on to the egg whites while continuing to whisk. The result will be a softer meringue which can be piped.

3. Soften the gelatine in cold water and add to the warm anglaise. Dissolve and strain.

4. Gently fold in the meringue and Drambuie.

5. Lightly fold in the cream.

Raspberry mousse

$3^{1}/_{2}$ leaves of gelatine
$^{1}/_{8}$pt (75ml) Italienne meringue
$^{1}/_{2}$pt (300ml) fresh raspberry purée
$^{1}/_{2}$pt (300ml) lightly whipped whipping cream

Same as for the Drambuie mousse, with raspberry purée substituted for sauce anglaise.

Raspberry glaze

1 Bramley apple, peeled and cored
$^{1}/_{4}$pt (150ml) stock syrup – $^{3}/_{4}$pt (450ml) water and 1lb (450g) sugar
   1 zest of lemon
$^{1}/_{4}$pt (150ml) raspberry purée
3 leaves of gelatine, softened

1. Gently poach the apple in the stock syrup with the lemon zest, then add the raspberry purée. Boil and skim.

2. Add the gelatine and dissolve, then gently pour off into muslin. Allow the liquid to drain, do not squeeze. Cool.

Biscuit
4oz (100–125g) butter
6oz (175g) caster sugar
4$^1/_2$oz (130g) egg white
6oz (175g) plain flour
vanilla to flavour

1. Cream the butter and sugar then slowly add the egg whites and finally mix in the flour and vanilla.
2. Spread the mixture over a thistle stencil and bake for 2–3 minutes.
3. Remove and, while still hot, form around a ring.

To serve the dish
Gently remove the cling film and release the mousse on to cold plates. Surround with the thistle biscuit and present with a little raspberry and mango sauces.

Iced pyramid of banana parfait centred with a pear sorbet served with a duo of sauces

SERVES 4

This dish was created as part of a three-course meal for the Egon Ronay British Port Competition.

banana parfait (see recipe below)
pear sorbet (see recipe below)
biscuit (see recipe below)
caramel sauce (see recipe below)
vanilla sauce (see recipe below)

1. Make banana parfait (see recipe below)
2. Make pear sorbet (see recipe below)
3. Make biscuit (see recipe below)
4. Make caramel sauce (see recipe below)
5. Make vanilla sauce (see recipe below)

Parfait
4oz (100-125g) caster sugar
$1/4$pt (150ml) water
5 egg yolks
$7^1/_2$ fl oz (210ml) milk
$1/4$pt (150ml) double cream
$1/2$ tsp vanilla essence, one vanilla pod or 3–4 drops vanilla extract
1 large banana, ripe
$1^1/_2$ measures banana liqueur

1. Boil the sugar and water until thick but do not colour.
2. Whisk the egg yolks until light, then slowly pour on the hot sugar. Continue to whisk.
3. Boil the milk, cream, vanilla, banana and liqueur and infuse for 5 minutes.
4. Pass through a fine sieve on to the egg mixture, whisking all the time.
5. Cool, then place in an ice-cream machine and freeze. Fill into 4 pyramid moulds and place in the freezer for 1 hour.

Pear sorbet

4oz (100–125g) caster sugar
$^1/_4$pt (150ml) cold water
2 pears, ripe
1 measure Poire William

1. Boil the sugar and water together. Remove and cool.
2. Peel the pears and core them and add to the syrup. Liquidise and pass through a fine sieve. Add the liqueur, then freeze in an ice-cream machine.
3. Remove and place in a freezer.
4. Scoop out the centre of the parfait and fill with the pear sorbet. Replace in the freezer until required.

Biscuit

10oz (300g) caster sugar
3 fl oz (75 ml) water
3oz (75g) toasted almonds

1. Boil the sugar and add water until a light caramel is formed. Mix in the almonds, then pour out on to a non-stick or oiled surface. Cool to a powder.
2. Sieve the powder over a template to form pyramid-shaped sides on a baking sheet. Bake in a hot oven at 300°F/150°C/Gas Mark 2 or until sugar melts and then remove and let cool.

Caramel sauce

2oz (50g) butter
3oz (75g) soft brown sugar
2oz (50g) golden syrup
1 tbsp condensed milk
8 fl oz (225ml) double cream
2 measures dark rum

1. Melt the butter, sugar, syrup, and condensed milk in a pan, then add the cream. Bring to the boil and strain. Finish with the rum. Cool. If too thick, add a little milk.

Vanilla sauce

17 fl oz (500ml) milk
1 vanilla pod
5 free-range egg yolks
3oz (75ml) caster sugar

1. Boil the milk with the split vanilla pod and infuse for 5 minutes.
2. Whisk the egg yolks and sugar until white. Add the milk and gently cook over a moderate heat until the sauce coats the back of a spoon. Strain and cool ready for use.

To serve the dish

Using a little chocolate, pipe two tear drops and fill with a little of each sauce. Remove the parfait and carefully extract from the mould. Place on to a plate and add the biscuit sides. A small amount of seasonal berries can be used along with caramelised orange zest to finish the dish.

CHAPTER EIGHT

KEITH AND NICOLA BRAIDWOOD

ONE of the most important things in cooking is not being alone in the kitchen. Everyone needs someone to bounce ideas off and discuss things with. A good kitchen isn't necessarily one with one boss. We work on a very equal basis, and we find that there is no ego. We are very unusual in that there are two people of equal rank in the kitchen. Yet we've never had a serious argument over food. We have the benefit of two opinions on each dish. We tend to sit down on Sunday night when the restaurant is closed and discuss food. Whatever we come up with might very well end up on the next week's menu.

We've become rather famous for our desserts, in particular our chocolate puddings and our chocolates. But this has tended to disguise the overall picture. We never intended to specialise in the pastry side – that was by accident more than design, more luck than anything else. The lucky thing was that we found most chefs lacked in-depth knowledge of pastry and chocolate work, and we had the opportunity to spend a great deal of time acquiring the skills and know-how that a great many chefs do not have.

Probably our first big breakthrough in public terms was doing the chocolate tear drop dessert for the first Scottish Food Proms Gala Dinner. We had been doing this dish for maybe a maximum of eight people on a busy night, and suddenly we had to do it for 250. It was daunting, but exciting at the same time. More importantly, it was successful and brought us a lot of publicity. After that, we entered competitions and worked on our skills, and all of a sudden we had a reputation for our desserts.

We work together on our desserts, as with all things, but we have our own set of influences – the lime parfait, for example, is all Nicola and the caramel mousse is all Keith. Perhaps a measure of how far we have come is that in the first three months of opening Braidwoods, we've sold over 100 boxes of chocolates for guests to take away and to people outside the restaurant.

Recipe ideas come in many sorts of different ways. Apart from our own food sessions, sometimes we'll see an idea that another chef has done and think we'd like to try to develop his or her idea in a different way. *Halibut with olives in a shellfish sauce* was an idea that we had developed after seeing something Shaun Hill at Gidleigh Park did with salmon, olives, shallots and a white-wine sauce. We wanted to use a meaty white fish rather than salmon. We preferred halibut, and we thought of a real olive topping rather than just plain olives. We wanted the olives to form a crust, and for that we needed a binding. Being a few miles away from the Isle of Arran we thought of using Arran mustard. We also added the herbs and we thought the shellfish sauce would be more interesting, since the colour added contrast.

Recognised as two of Scotland's best younger chefs, **KEITH AND NICOLA BRAIDWOOD** set up Braidwoods in Dalry in Ayrshire in July 1994 after running the kitchen in Shieldhill at Biggar. They had previously worked together under Bruce Sangster at Murrayshall Hotel in Perthshire. Keith, who is 28, started his career as a commis chef at the Peat Inn, Fife, and subsequently worked at Inverlochy Castle, Mallory Court in Leamington Spa and the Royal Oak at Yattendon. Nicola, who is 26, studied at Lancaster and Morecambe College before going on placement to the Royal Oak.

Caesar salad with avocado and smoked chicken

SERVES 8

We had the chance to taste many different versions of the Caesar salad on a recent trip to California. Most of them were pretty average, using additional ingredients like chargrilled chicken breast and a little anchovy flavour. This is our version.

1 tin anchovies
2 cloves garlic
juice of 1 lemon
2 tbsp mayonnaise
3 fl oz (75ml) olive oil
3 tbsp cold water
2 Romaine lettuce
croutons
8 cherry tomatoes
1 smoked chicken
2 avocadoes
4oz (100–125g) fresh Parmesan

1. First make the dressing. In a blender, combine the anchovies, garlic, lemon juice and mayonnaise. Slowly add the olive oil and adjust with a little cold water. Season to taste.
2. Chop up the lettuce roughly and toss with the croutons, tomatoes and dressing.
3. Cut the smoked chicken into slices. Slice the avocado.
4. Shave the fresh Parmesan using a potato peeler.

To serve the dish
Divide the chicken and avocado between the eight plates, interleaving chicken and avocado in a fan-shape. Pile the lettuce mixture on top. Sprinkle the Parmesan shavings on top of the lettuce mixture.

Cream of courgette and Bonchester cheese soup

SERVES 6–8

This is a very simple soup with a rich flavour and lovely colour. The only caution is not to overcook. The secret is to blend the ingredients and then cool them down quickly in iced water so that the soup keeps its green colour. Reheat as you need it – do not keep warm as the soup will turn brown.

1lb (450g) courgettes
2oz (50g) onion
2oz (50g) leek
chives
$2^1/_2$ (60g) butter
1oz (25g) plain flour
$2^1/_2$pt ($1^1/_2$l) chicken stock (see recipe below)
1 small Bonchester cheese (about 6oz/140g)
$^1/_8$pt (75ml) double cream

1. Chop the courgettes, the onion, leek and chives.
2. Heat up the stock.
3. Sweat the onion and leek in butter for a couple of minutes.
4. Add flour and cook on a low-to-medium heat for a few minutes, stirring all the time.
5. Add the chopped courgettes and cook for a few minutes.
6. Add the hot stock. Season.
7. Simmer for 15–20 minutes. Blend in a food blender and pass through a fine sieve. Then cool this down quickly in iced water.
8. Cut up the Bonchester.
9. Heat the soup and add the cream. Check seasoning.

Chicken stock

carcases of 3 chickens with skins and fat removed, and washed and
    drained
1 large carrot, quartered
2 med. leeks and 2 sticks of celery all halved lengthwise
1 onion with skin on quartered
1 small bulb garlic halved
6 white peppercorns
1 bay leaf
1 sprig thyme
$^1/_2$oz (15g) parsley or tarragon stalks

1. Place carcases into a large pot (large enough so that the bones only
   take up half of the depth of pot), cover them completely with cold
   water and bring to the boil.
2. Once boiling hard, skim off all of the scum and fat from the surface
   using a skimmer. Reduce the heat and simmer for 3 hours.
3. Remove from heat and empty contents into a colander set over a
   bowl.
4. Pass the stock through a chinois into a tall polypropylene container
   or pint jug and allow to cool by placing container into a sink of cold
   water.
5. When cool, place in fridge overnight until fat settles on top. Skim off
   fat and spoon out jellied stock into tubs and freeze immediately.

NOTE
1. In summer it is best to freeze stock immediately, while in winter it
   will keep for up to 48 hours in the fridge.
2. Good fish and chicken stock should form a slight jelly consistency.
3. Always make stock in advance and freeze, making as large a quantity
   as possible at a time.
4. Always cut whole garlic heads across their 'equators'.

To serve the dish

Put the pieces of Bonchester cheese in the bottom of the soup bowls. Pour the
soup into the bowls and garnish with the croutons and the chopped chives.

Loin of roe deer in a wild-mushroom custard and a thyme essence

SERVES 4

The origins of this dish go back to when Keith started working at the Peat Inn as a commis chef at the age of 17. One of the first dishes he was allowed to make was the mushroom ramekin. It has remained in his head ever since, although we have substituted wild mushrooms for field in this recipe. This is an excellent dish for eating at home as most of the work is done in advance and the actual cooking of the venison takes hardly any time at all. We call the wild-mushroom part a 'baked custard' because it is made with eggs and double cream.

6oz mixed wild mushrooms
red-wine-and-port-and-madeira sauce (see recipe below)
$^{1}/_{2}$oz (15g) butter
1 egg yolk
$^{1}/_{4}$pt (150ml) double cream
seasoning
4x5oz (150g) boned loin of roe deer

1. Peel and roughly chop the mushrooms. Keep the mushroom skins and other trimmings for the sauce.
2. Make the red-wine-and-port-and-madeira sauce (see recipe below).
3. Sweat the mushrooms in butter in a pan until all the liquid has evaporated. Leave to cool.
4. Whisk together the egg yolk and the cream and season. Add the cool mushrooms to this mix.
5. Line 4 small moulds with cling film and divide the mix equally between them.
6. Butter some foil and use to cover the moulds. Cook in a bain-marie on 325°F/170°C/Gas Mark 3 until the mould is just setting.
7. Seal off the roe deer, seasoning both sides.
8. Roast the deer in a high oven 425°F/220°C/Gas Mark 7 for about 5 minutes or longer, depending on how you like the meat cooked.

Red-wine-and-port-and-madeira sauce

1 carrot
2 shallots
2 garlic cloves
$^1/_2$ onion
$^1/_2$ leek
8oz (225g) chopped game bones
$^1/_2$ bottle red wine
1 fl oz (25ml) red-wine vinegar
2 fl oz (50ml) port
wild mushroom trimmings
4 sprigs thyme
$^1/_2$pt (300ml) good game stock
2 fl oz (50ml) madeira
2oz (50g) butter

1. Chop the carrot, shallots, garlic, onion and leek.
2. In a hot pan, brown the game bones.
3. Add the chopped vegetables and brown off.
4. Add the red wine, red-wine vinegar, port, mushroom trimmings and thyme. Reduce by half.
5. Add game stock and again reduce by half. Check seasoning.
6. Pass the sauce through a fine sieve or muslin cloth.
7. Add the madeira.
8. Thicken the sauce with the butter and add some thyme leaves if required.

To serve the dish

Turn out the mushroom from the moulds on to the plate. The mushroom will sit on the plate like custard. Carve the roe around. Spoon the sauce around the meat.

Gressingham duck with a cranberry-and-ginger essence

SERVES 4

The duck leg is our biggest seller and can be used as a starter as well as a main course. The meat just falls off the bone, just like crispy duck in a good Chinese restaurant.

4 Gressingham preserved duck legs (see recipe below)
1 carrot
1 onion
1 leek
1oz (25g) fresh ginger
8oz (225g) duck bones
$^1\!/_2$oz (15g) sugar
1 sprig thyme
$^1\!/_4$pt (150ml) red wine
$^1\!/_2$pt (300ml) fresh orange juice
1pt (600ml) dark duck stock (jelly)
4 Gressingham duck breasts
sea salt
pepper
1 tbsp honey
2oz (50g) fresh cranberries
1oz (25g) unsalted butter

1. Preserve duck legs at least 2 days in advance (see recipe below).
2. Chop carrot, onion, leek and ginger.
3. Brown off duck bones in a pan and add chopped vegetables. Sweat off vegetables, pour in the sugar and all the mix to caramelise.
4. Add thyme and ginger.
5. Mix the red wine and the orange juice and add to the mixture. Reduce sauce by half.
6. Slowly add the duck stock to the mixture, while all the time reducing the sauce again by half and skimming off excess scum.
7. Remove the sauce from heat and pass through a fine sieve.
8. Now remove the duck legs from the fat and heat in a hot oven until the skin starts to crisp.

9. Now take the duck breasts and with a sharp knife score the fatty side of the breasts in criss-cross fashion. Season the duck breasts, then seal in a hot frying-pan until the skin is golden brown.
10. Remove the duck breasts from the pan and spread honey over the fatty part of the breast.
11. Put the breasts under a hot grill and continue cooking until the fat is crisp but not burned.
12. Reduce the sauce by half and add cranberries. Thicken with knobs of the butter.

Preserved duck leg

4 duck legs
$^1/_2$pt (300ml) duck or pork fat rendered/melted (which you can buy from your butcher)
1 onion
1 carrot
1 shallot
1 clove garlic
2 bay leaves
1 sprig thyme
1 sprig tarragon
1 sliced orange
crushed black pepper
salt
4 cloves
2 star anise
2 pinches of Chinese five spice

1. Place all the ingredients in a pan with a tight-fitting lid and cook for $3^1/_2$ hours at 300°F/150°C/Gas Mark 2.
2. Remove the duck legs from the pan and sieve the fat over them. Allow the duck legs to cool.
3. Place the duck legs in a bowl and pour the fat over them. Place the bowl in the fridge and keep there for at least 2 days.

To serve the dish

Carve the breast and fan slices around the duck leg. Sauce the dish and serve with gratin potatoes.

Halibut with olives in a shellfish sauce

SERVES 4

This dish was inspired by Shaun Hill, formerly the head chef at Gidleigh Park. We serve this in the restaurant with caper potato cakes and a tagliatelli of carrot and courgette. If you don't want to use halibut, most other meaty fish would be a good substitute.

$^{1}/_{2}$oz ((15g) chives
$^{1}/_{2}$oz (15g) parsley
2 shallots
3oz pitted quality black olives
1 tsp Arran mustard
1oz (25g) fresh white breadcrumbs
1 tbsp olive oil
seasoning
shellfish sauce (see recipe below)
1oz (25g) cold diced butter
4 x 5oz (150g) pieces of halibut fillet

1. Chop the chives and the parsley and finely chop the shallots.
2. Quarter the olives. Put in a bowl and add the chopped chives, chopped parsley, shallots, mustard, breadcrumbs, olive oil and seasoning. Refrigerate until needed.
3. Make the shellfish sauce (see recipe below).
4. Butter a metal baking tray and place the halibut fillets on it. Add seasoning.
5. The olive mixture is to act as a topping to the halibut, so divide the topping into four and spoon the mixture over the top of each fillet. Gently press the topping down evenly.
6. Butter some tinfoil and use it to cover the fillets with olive topping.
7. Bake the fillets in the oven at 425°F/220°C/Gas Mark 7 for 4–5 minutes.
8. Now heat the shellfish sauce in a pan and bring to the boil. Add the butter to thicken the sauce. Check the seasoning.

Bruce Sangster
ICED PYRAMID OF BANANA PARFAIT CENTRED WITH A PEAR SORBET
SERVED WITH A DUO OF SAUCES

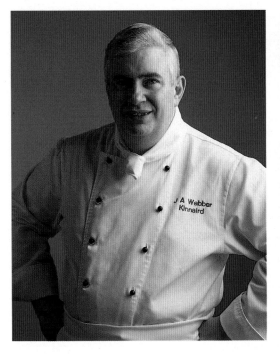

JOHN WEBBER

BRUCE SANGSTER

KEITH AND NICOLA BRAIDWOOD

Keith and Nicola Braidwood
HALIBUT WITH OLIVES IN A SHELLFISH SAUCE

John Webber

FILO-PASTRY FLAN OF COURGETTE AND TOMATO SEASONED WITH FETA CHEESE AND BASIL

Shellfish sauce
1 carrot
1 stick of celery
$^1/_2$ onion
$^1/_4$ fennel
1 star anise
1 tbsp olive oil
$^1/_2$lb (225g) langoustine heads (or lobster shells)
1 tbsp tomato purée
$^1/_4$pt (150ml) dry white wine
$^1/_2$pt (300ml) fish stock (see recipe below)
4 fl oz (100ml) double cream

1. Roughly chop the carrot, the onion and the fennel. Crush the star anise.
2. Heat the olive oil in a thick-bottomed pan until it is very hot, and fry the shells until dry.
3. Add the chopped vegetables and star anise and continue frying for about 5 minutes.
4. Add the tomato purée and the white wine.
5. Simmer until the sauce is reduced by half.
6. Add the fish stock and reduce by half again.
7. Add the cream and bring back to the boil.
8. Remove from heat and pass through a fine sieve, discarding the shells and vegetables and keeping the liquid.
9. Set the sauce aside until the fish is almost cooked.

Fish stock
$1^1/_2$lb (675g) of fish bones (preferably sole, turbot or brill)
$^1/_2$ medium onion
1 white leek
$^1/_2$ bulb fennel
1 stick celery
6 white peppercorns
$^1/_2$ bay leaf
$^1/_2$oz (15g) fresh herbs or stalks -chervil, parsley, tarragon and coriander
1 tbsp olive oil
$^1/_2$pt (300ml) dry white wine

1. Soak the fish bones for one hour, then drain, wash and chop them.
2. Finely dice the vegetables.
3. Gently sweat all the vegetables, peppercorns, bay leaf and herbs in the olive oil until soft but without colouring. Add white wine and boil until nearly dry, then add fish bones and stir to coat.
4. Add enough cold water to cover ingredients, bring to the boil, skim and simmer for 18 minutes. Then remove from heat and allow to stand until cool.
5. Once cool, pour stock through a sieve or colander, then pass through a chinois into a tall container. Place in the fridge overnight and next day spoon off all of the clear jelly on the top. This should then be frozen in small containers.

To serve the dish
Pour the shellfish sauce on to the plate and place the halibut with olive topping on top.

Caramel mousse

SERVES 6

This dish has been on various menus where we have worked since 1989. It formed part of the dessert we did for 250 people at the Scottish Food Proms Gala Dinner in Glasgow last year. The dish is so popular, it will probably still be on our menus until we hang up our aprons.

11 fl oz (325ml) double cream
5 eggs, separated
2 leaves of gelatine
4$^{1}/_{2}$oz (140g) caster sugar
$^{1}/_{2}$ tbsp lemon juice
1oz (25g) toasted almonds
crème anglaise (optional – see recipe below)

1. Whip 10 fl oz (300ml) of the cream to ribbon stage. Set to one side.
2. Use a machine to beat yolks in a bowl until white.
3. Soak gelatine in cold water to soften it.
4. Place sugar, lemon juice and gelatined water in a pan. Bring to the boil and continue boiling until it reaches caramel stage.
5. Once at the caramel stage, pour carefully and slowly on to the yolks in the bowl and keep mixing until cool.
6. Warm the remaining 1 fl oz (25ml) of double cream. Dissolve softened gelatine into it. Stir until dissolved.
7. Now add this mixture to the egg yolks.
8. Pour the mixture into ramekins or moulds. Refrigerate.
9. Toast the almonds until lightly brown.

Crème anglaise
$^{1}/_{2}$pt (300ml) milk
1 tbsp double cream
$^{1}/_{2}$ vanilla pod, split
4 egg yolks
2oz (50g) caster sugar

1. Place milk, cream and vanilla pod in a pan and bring to the boil.
2. Whisk yolks and sugar together.

3. Pour milk mixture on to yolk mixture, whisking all the time.
4. Pour this new mixture into a clean pan, and at a medium heat slowly bring back to heat, stirring continuously until it is thick enough to coat the back of a spoon.
5. Remove pan from heat and sieve.
6. Continue stirring until mixture is cool. Be careful not to beat too vigorously or the mixture will split.

To serve this dish
Take out the ramekins from the refrigerator 20 minutes before serving and allow them to come up to room temperature. Decorate with the whipped cream and toasted almonds. Or serve with the crème anglaise.

Coffee-and-brandy truffles

MAKES 30–40 TRUFFLES

Make no bones about it, this is messy and time-consuming but well worth it. The secret is to take your time. Keith spent a week in Holland with one of their top chocolatiers, and he has always had a great reputation for chocolate work. Truffles make a change from the tablet which most Scottish restaurants seem to offer as petits four. If you persevere with this recipe, you will find that the truffles are a great conversation piece for your dinner guests. In any case, everyone loves chocolate, so all your hard work will be welcomed by your guests.

1lb (450g) good-quality milk chocolate (obtainable from most good delicatessens)
$^1/_2$lb (225g) Bournville plain chocolate
$^1/_2$pt (300ml) double cream
1 tsp instant coffee
1 tbsp brandy
2oz (50g) unsalted butter
2oz (50ml) liquid glucose (obtainable from health-food shops and some chemists)

1. Make sure you have your piping bag (with plain nozzle) and three small trays lined with grease-proof paper ready before you start.
2. The first thing to work on is the filling. Chop $^1/_2$lb (225g) of the milk chocolate and all of the Bournville as small as possible.
3. Select a thick-bottomed pan and put into it the cream, coffee, brandy, butter and glucose. Slowly bring to the boil.
4. Once boiled, take the mixture off the heat and immediately stir in the chocolate thoroughly.
5. Leave the mixture to cool naturally, stirring occasionally. At this stage, it is important to resist the temptation to put the mixture into the fridge, as you will end up with a split mixture at the piping stage. Ideally, you should let the mixture cool overnight.
6. When the mixture is stone cold, whisk it with an electric mixer until it goes pale and thickens. This does not take long.
7. Spoon the mixture into a piping bag. Lay out the trays lined with grease-proof paper. Pipe the mixture on to the trays.
8. Refrigerate the trays for an hour.
9. While the trays are in the fridge, place the Bournville in a bowl over a pan of water. Gently heat the water. Once again take your time. Be patient. It is important not to allow the melting Bournville to get hot – it should be warm, no hotter than blood heat – otherwise the truffle will melt when it is dipped in this mixture.
10. When the chocolate is melted, remove the bowl from the pan and set the chocolate mixture aside to cool.
11. Grate the remaining $^1/_2$lb (225g) milk chocolate and scatter on a tray.
12. Once the truffles are set, remove from refrigerator.
13. Lift up each truffle with a fork and dip it into the melted Bournville, and then roll the Bournville-coated truffle on the tray or grated milk chocolate until the truffle is thoroughly coated with milk chocolate.
14. Place the coated truffles on to grease-proof paper on a tray.
15. If you are not planning to serve the truffles immediately, then you need to store them in an airtight container in the fridge – there should be grease-proof paper between each layer of truffles. They will keep for a week in the fridge.

Lime parfait with a caramelised orange syrup

SERVES 12

This is a lovely dish, but we need to sound a word of caution. When making the parfait, be careful not to over-whip the cream. Also, make sure the orange juice and zest are hot before the sugar reaches the caramel stage. You may add more lime if the flavour is not strong enough for your taste.

1pt (600ml) double cream
juice and zest of 4 limes
4 eggs
5oz (150g) caster sugar
8oz (225g) sugar
2 tbsp water
juice and zest of 2 oranges
orange segments

1. Whip the double cream to ribbon stage. Add the lime zest and juice. Set to one side.
2. Separate the eggs. Whip up the yolks on a machine until white, then add the caster sugar gradually.
3. Whip the egg whites.
4. Add the cream to the yolk mixture and carefully fold in. Then fold in the egg whites thoroughly.
5. Line a terrine mould (or ramekins) with cling film and pour this mixture in. Place in the freezer for 4 hours or until frozen.
6. Boil the sugar and water to caramel stage.
7. Warm the orange juice and zest in a pan.
8. Whisk the caramel slowly and carefully on to the orange juice and zest. Leave to cool and you will have your orange syrup.

To serve this dish
Turn out the parfait on to a tray and slice with a hot knife. Put a slice of parfait and a spoonful of orange syrup on to the plate. Decorate with three segments of fresh orange, which helps cut through the sweetness of the sauce.

CHAPTER NINE

JOHN WEBBER

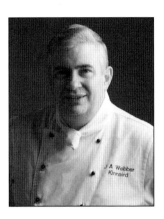

I ALWAYS find that my surroundings influence my thinking and, likewise, my style of cooking. Some years ago, I decided to specialise in the country-house market. I like to work with ingredients in which pure flavours are prominent, and I found this simplicity mirrored in the direct, informal approach of country-house cooking.

The recipes that I have presented here all concentrate on pure flavour. The filo-pastry flan is very light and contains a fragrant bite as you find the pesto. It is ideal for vegetarians and can be slipped into a menu to break up and alter the pace of a meal. The pasta, on the other hand, is full bodied, with robust flavour and textures. Both the scallops and the salmon have a lighter touch, with refreshing dressings to complement the fish. They can either form an outdoor lunch or be incorporated into a dinner menu.

The lamb shanks represent my favourite type of food: earthy and robust without being heavy. The pea mousse recalls the mushy-pea stalls of Great Yarmouth. The venison, too, brings back memories: it was specially designed for one of the first Scottish Food Proms, where it proved to be a winner, and it has since become a standard dish in the restaurant.

To finish, I have included two fruity desserts, although they are very different from one another. The mulled fruits again provide a full-bodied flavour. The fruits, all but one dried, see us through the winter and provide a warming finish to the meal. The glazed fruits, on the other hand, show off the best of the summer fruits, with added flavour from the wine and sorbet.

JOHN WEBBER came to Scotland after a highly successful career as head chef at Gidleigh Park in Devon and the famous Cliveden. He has won considerable acclaim for his cooking at Kinnaird and is on the advisory board of the Scottish Chefs Association.

Filo-pastry flan of courgette and tomato seasoned with feta cheese and basil

SERVES 4

This dish is very versatile. It can be served as a vegetarian dish or as an accompaniment to a main course. Or it can be a small appetiser. It's relatively easy to do and it's a light dish. Last year it was served to 250 people at the Scottish Food Proms Gala Dinner in Glasgow.

4 sheets filo pastry
good quality olive oil
6 tomatoes, plum if possible
4 courgettes
garlic
sea-salt
mill pepper
4 dessertspoons pesto sauce (see recipe below)
6oz (175g) feta cheese
1oz (25g) pine kernels
basil

1. Carefully unwrap the filo pastry and lay it out on to a flat surface and cover with a cloth to avoid the paste drying out. Personally, I prefer a frozen brand of filo, which is less liable to crack and dry out. Avoid any which has been tightly folded in packaging.
2. Take the first sheet off the stack. Place alongside and brush lightly with the olive oil. Cover with another sheet of pastry and repeat until you have a piece of pastry three layers thick and covered in oil.
3. Cut out disks of pastry using a saucer or small plate about 5in. (12$\frac{1}{2}$cm) diameter, cutting around with the point of a sharp knife. Arrange the disks on a baking sheet and put aside.
4. Blanch, peel and de-seed the tomatoes. Cut the flesh into $\frac{1}{4}$in. ($\frac{1}{2}$cm) dice and set aside. A very handy way of removing the skin from the tomato is to use a gas blowtorch similar to the type used by plumbers. Simply remove the core of the tomato with the point of a knife, spike the fruit on a fork and run the flame quickly over the skin. The skin will blister and peel off easily – the same will happen to your skin, given the chance, so be careful and turn the torch off as soon as you have finished.

5. Top, tail and wash the courgettes. Then slice them into $^1/_8$in. (3mm) thick rounds. Pour some of the oil into a large shallow pan and half-cook the slices by tossing in the hot oil with a clove of garlic for flavour. Spread the cooked courgette on to a tray and allow to cool.

6. Arrange the courgette on the filo discs in concentric circles, starting $^1/_4$in. ($^1/_2$cm) in from the edge and overlapping each slice slightly until the disc is covered.

7. Place $^1/_2$oz (15g) of tomato in the centre of each disc and season the flan with salt and mill pepper. Coat the tomato with a quarter of the pesto sauce, and place a further $^1/_2$oz (15g) of tomato on top.

8. Divide the cheese between the flans and sprinkle with pine kernels.

9. Bake in an oven at 400°F/200°C/Gas Mark 6 for about 8 minutes.

Pesto sauce
1 medium garlic clove
$1^1/_2$oz (40g) Parmesan cheese
2oz (50g) fresh basil leaves
$1^1/_2$oz (40g) pine kernels
$^1/_4$ tsp salt
3 fl oz (75 ml) good olive oil

1. Peel the garlic and freshly grate the Parmesan.
2. Place all the ingredients except the oil in your food processor fitted with the cutting blade. Process until a purée is formed.
3. Continue to blend while adding the oil in a thin stream.
4. Stop the processor, lift off the lid and scrape down the mixture from the sides of the bowl.
5. Blend again so that all the ingredients are evenly mixed.
6. Scrape out into a jamjar and cover until required. It will keep for several weeks if refrigerated. The colour may change a little but it will still taste sensational. A little goes a long way and can also be used to liven up pasta, risotto and vegetables, etc.

To serve the dish
Garnish with freshly cut basil.

Open ravioli of pigeon breast with red wine, lentils and smoked bacon

SERVES 4

A lot of the work in this dish can be done in advance. It has a good strong flavour, the combination of pigeon meat, the lentils, bacon and the sauce.

4 wood pigeons
thyme leaves
orange zest
olive oil
1oz (30g) each carrot, celery, shallot
4 fl oz (100ml) red wine (Cabernet Sauvignon)
4 fl oz (100ml) chicken stock
$^1/_2$pt (300ml) beef stock
2 juniper berries
1 sprig thyme
$^1/_2$oz (15g) redcurrant jelly
arrowroot
3oz (75g) cooked lentil du Puy
$1^1/_2$oz (40g) smoked bacon (cut in $^3/_4$in. x $1^1/_2$in./2cm x 4cm strips)
8 pasta squares, 35 x 35in. (90 x 90cm)
4oz (100-125g) fresh chanterelle (small if possible)

1. Using a very sharp knife, remove the breasts from the pigeons without the wing bones but leaving the skin on.
2. Sprinkle the breasts with fresh thyme leaves, thinly cut orange zest and olive oil. Leave the breasts to absorb the flavours for at least a couple of hours or up to two days in the refrigerator.
3. Using a large knife, roughly chop half of the bones and legs. Take a thick-based frying pan and brown the bones evenly in a little oil. Lift out the bones into a colander and repeat the process with the vegetables.
4. Swill out the pan with the red wine, collecting all the juices and pour them into a stainless-steel saucepan. Add the chicken and beef stock to the wine, add the bones and vegetables and bring slowly to the simmer, removing any scum that forms.
5. Slowly simmer the sauce for 35 minutes, then add the crushed juniper berries and thyme branch. Simmer for a further 10 minutes, then strain off the liquid

and pass through a muslin cloth. Add the redcurrant jelly and return to the heat in a clean pan and simmer until a good flavour is obtained (the liquid will have reduced by roughly half).

6.   Lightly thicken with dilute arrowroot, cover and set aside.

All of the work to this point may be done in advance, even the day before, but the following stages must be completed when the dish is to be served.

7.   Heat a frying-pan with a heavy base, and fry the pigeon breasts in a little of the oil they have been standing in. Cook the breasts skin-side down for 2-3 minutes, then turn over and cook for a further 2 minutes. The breasts should be kept underdone to enjoy the meat at its best. (Cooking the pigeon on a chargrill if you have one will add an extra dimension to the flavours.) Place the cooked meat on a warm plate and allow the meat to relax without cooking.

8.   Return the sauce to the stove and bring up to the simmer, add the bacon and cooked lentils and simmer for 2 minutes, removing any scum that forms.

9.   Cook the pasta squares in boiling salted water with a drop of oil. Timing will depend upon the type of pasta used, but for homemade fresh pasta 4 minutes should do. Drain the pasta and return to the pan with a drop of olive oil and seasonings.

10. To serve the ravioli quickly, sauté the wild mushrooms in a little olive oil for 3 minutes. Add about a dessertspoon of water to the hot pan to stop the mushrooms overcooking and keep warm.

To serve the dish

Take a deep plate and place one of the pasta squares in the centre. Lift a little of the lentils and bacon from the sauce and dress on the pasta. Remove the skin from the pigeon and thinly slice the breasts. Place the slices on the bed of lentils and surround with sauce. Arrange the second sheet of pasta on top of the pigeon and divide the cooked mushrooms between the plates, placing them around the pasta. Crispy fried celeriac strips may be used as an optional garnish.

Braised lamb shank served with a minted-pea mousse

SERVES 4

This great winter dish combines rich and piquant flavours in a very robust and hearty dish. The shanks will benefit from being cooked the day before.

4 lamb shanks
4oz (100–125g) dried split peas
1 carrot
1 medium onion
2 rashers smoked back bacon
bay leaf
thyme branch
3oz (75g) each of sliced carrot, shallot and celery
1 clove of garlic
4 small sprigs rosemary
1$^{1}/_{2}$pt (900ml) light beef stock
1 tsp tomato purée
$^{1}/_{2}$pt (300ml) white wine
arrowroot
prepared mint sauce
8 lamb cutlets
glazed vegetables to garnish
wild mushrooms

1. The day before, place the dried peas in a colander and wash well under running water. Transfer to a bowl and cover with cold water to a depth of one inch and allow to stand overnight.
2. When buying the lamb shanks, ask the butcher to saw off one inch from the thin end of the shank and to carefully saw off the knuckle end without removing too much meat – but remember to take the off-cuts home with you.
3. Drain off the soaked peas in a colander and wash well. Place them into a large pot and add water to cover with about 2in. (5cm) of water above the peas. Add the carrot and onion whole, the bacon rashers and the herbs.
4. Bring to the simmer and skim off the scum. Lower the heat and simmer very gently for 4 hours, stirring frequently.
5. Heat a large frying-pan. Add a little cooking oil and fry the shanks to a

golden brown colour. Remove from the pan and transfer them to a deep pot suitable for the oven. Fry the off-cuts in the same way, add the carrot, shallot and celery and then add to the shanks once the vegetables have achieved a light colour.

6. Thinly slice the garlic clove, then wrap each shank together with a slice of garlic and a sprig of rosemary in a square of muslin. Tie the ends and return to the pan. This will ensure that the shanks do not break up during cooking.

7. Now add the beef stock, tomato purée and white wine to the pan and bring to the simmer. Cover with a lid and cook in a medium oven for $2^1/4$ hours, a little longer if the shanks are large.

8. Carefully remove the shanks but do not unwrap. Strain the sauce then pass through muslin into a clean pan. Return to the stove and bring up to the simmer, skimming off any scum that might appear.

9. Allow the sauce to reduce at a simmer until a good flavour is achieved (roughly a third to a half), then thicken lightly with the arrowroot diluted with water.

10. The pea mousse should now be very thick and have become almost a purée. Remove the vegetables and herbs but leave the bacon in. Pass the mixture through a coarse sieve and return to the heat in a clean pan. The mixture should be cooked very gently until it will stand up on its own. Stir in the mint sauce and correct the seasonings.

11. Season the lamb cutlets and grill, keeping the meat pink. Reheat the garnishing vegetables in a little butter and sugar until hot and glazed, and mould the pea mousse into buttered timbales (reheat in a water bath if the mousse has cooled off).

12. Unwrap the shanks and carefully reheat in the finished sauce. Quickly fry the mushrooms in a little olive oil and season.

To serve the dish
Take four deep plates and place one shank in each. Pour some of the sauce over each shank and place two cutlets on each plate. Garnish with the pea mousse turned out of its mould and the hot vegetables and mushrooms. The dish is a complete meal in itself, and all that may be required to serve alongside are a few baked or sautéed potatoes if you wish.

Grilled fillet of salmon filled with apple and basil set on a light-vegetable dressing

SERVES 4

Whereas meat and fruit is a traditional combination, the marriage of fish and fruit is somewhat more unusual. However, it works extremely well, particularly with oily fish such as salmon.

1oz (25g) french beans
1oz (25g) courgettes
1oz (25g) carrot
1oz (25g) tomato flesh
1 spring onion, finely sliced
$^2/_5$oz (10g) dill leaf
$^2/_5$oz (10g) each, onion, carrot, celery
1 bay leaf
1 sprig thyme
$^1/_2$ clove garlic
1oz (30g) dry white wine
$^1/_5$oz (5g) peeled lemon zest
$^1/_5$oz (5g) peeled orange zest
4oz (100–125g) fruity virgin olive oil
3 apples
1oz (25g) butter
juice of $^1/_2$ lemon
basil
4 x 5 oz (150g) wild-salmon fillet portions with skin on
1oz (25g) frozen, skinned broad beans
sea-salt, mill pepper, nutmeg
lemon juice
11oz (300g) picked fresh spinach
$^1/_2$oz (15g) unsalted butter

Dice the french beans, the courgettes (skin on) and the carrot in $^1/_8$in. (4mm) dice and the tomato flesh in $^1/_4$in. (6mm) dice. Finely slice the spring onion and chop the dill leaf. Leave all this to one side.
To prepare the oil, thinly slice each of the 10g of onion, carrot and celery and place in a stainless-steel pan with the herbs, garlic, white wine, lemon zest,

orange zest, and olive oil. Bring to the simmer and hold at 180°F/80°C/Gas Mark low for 1 hour.

3. Peel, core and cut the apples into $^1/_4$in. (6mm) dice and gently cook for 2 minutes in the butter and lemon juice. Allow to cool and fold in the basil cut in thin strips.

4. Place the salmon fillet skin-side down on a chopping-board. Using a very sharp, thin-bladed knife, make a cut into the fish at an angle of 30 degrees across the width of the fillet.

5. Pull back the flesh and make a second cut in the opposite direction. You should now have something similar to the flaps on the back of an envelope. Holding the flaps back, fill the fillet with the cooked apple, mounding up the filling. Fold the flaps back around the apple. Brush with oil and refrigerate.

6. Blanch each of the diced vegetables separately in boiling salted water for 2 minutes and refresh under cold water.

7. Pour the olive oil into a bowl lined with muslin cloth. Hang the cloth above the bowl with a meat hook and allow to drain lightly, squeezing the cloth to remove all of the oil and juices. Add the diced vegetables to the oil, then add the chopped spring onion, tomato, herbs and beans. Correct the seasoning and add the lemon juice as needed.

8. Grill the fish, allowing the apples to brown and crispen slightly.

9. Wash the picked spinach and cook in a hot pan with the butter. No water will be needed.

To serve the dish

Season with the salt, pepper and nutmeg, and divide between four large hot plates, forming a nest in the centre of the plate for the fish to sit on. Give the fish a final brush with butter and set upon the spinach. Spoon the warmed oil with the vegetables around the fish and decorate with fresh herbs if required.

Sautéed scallop salad with a dressing of carrot and Sauternes

SERVES 4

This dish takes the traditional blend of carrots and Sauternes to form a light dressing for grilled scallops that complements the shellfish without masking the essence of the seafood. The recipe here is for a starter, but it would also make a good lunch dish if served with a tossed leaf salad.

12 hand-dived scallops
11oz (325g) carrot
15 fl oz (450ml) vegetable stock
5oz (150ml) Sauternes wine
1 cucumber
2 sprigs dill leaf
6 plum tomatoes
$^1/_2$oz (15g) yellow mustard seed (soaked in white wine overnight)
2 fl oz (50ml) olive-oil vinaigrette
juice of $^1/_2$ lemon
$^1/_2$oz (15g) unsalted butter
olive oil

1 Always try to buy scallops in the shell to guarantee freshness. Refuse any that are open and do not close when tapped on the table. Very often you will see scallops sitting in water in the fishmongers. Avoid these if you can, as the fish will absorb water and become soft and pappy. They also, of course, become heavier so never buy by weight. To open the scallops, hold the scallop in a cloth to protect your hands. Insert an old knife in the gap between the shells and release the flesh from the shell. An old table knife is ideal as it does not need to be sharp and is much safer should you slip. Remove the flat shell and then release the fish from the curved shell it is sitting in. Be careful not to waste any fish. Slide the fish into a bowl and remove the frilly skirt and membrane surrounding the white meat. The fish may twitch slightly in your hands. Don't worry as this is a sign of freshness, but it can be alarming at first. Retain the pink-and-white coloured roe and, of course, the white nut of meat but discard the rest.

2. Wash the scallop under running water for 2 seconds to remove any grit and place on a clean cloth to dry. On no account allow the fish to stand in water.

160

The pink roe is not required for this dish but can be frozen for use in salads or fish mousses.

3. Slice each nut of meat in half and refrigerate.

4. To make the dressing, dice 5oz (150g) of carrot and grate the remaining 6oz (175g). Simmer the diced carrot in the wine for 4 minutes and set aside. Simmer the grated carrot in the vegetable stock for 6 minutes, remove from the heat and allow to infuse for 30 minutes.

5. Pour the vegetable stock and carrot mixture into a bowl lined with muslin. Allow to drain and squeeze the cloth to remove all of the juices. The resulting liquid will look like carrot juice. Set aside for later. (Both of the operations for the dressing may be done the day before and finished when serving the dish.)

6. Take the cucumber and cut off each end, cut into $^1/_6$in. (2mm) slices and then into $^1/_6$in. (2mm) strips the length of the cucumber, avoiding the seeds. This will be much easier if you are lucky enough to have a mandolin slicer in the kitchen.

7. Cook the strips in boiling salted water for 30 seconds then refresh in ice-cold water, drain well and dry on a cloth.

8. Toss the dried cucumber in a little of the vinaigrette, season and mix in the dill leaf roughly chopped.

9. Remove the skin from the tomatoes. (See the filo-flan recipe for the best way to do this.) Dice the tomato flesh into $^1/_4$in. (6mm) shapes or diamonds. In a second bowl toss the diced tomato flesh with the mustard seeds and vinaigrette and season.

11. We are now ready to finish the dish. Return the carrot stock to the stove in a stainless-steel pan and boil down until only one-third remains. Add the diced-carrot mixture to this and boil for 3 minutes, remove from the heat and add the lemon juice then add in the firm butter.

12. Take a cast-iron or black-steel frying-pan and put on to full heat. Roll the scallops in olive oil and place in the hot pan. Sear on each side for 20 seconds (slightly longer if the fish is very thick) then remove from the pan to a warm plate. The pan must be very hot and no other fat will be required. Cooking the fish in this way will produce the best colour and flavour and the smell will certainly make you hungry.

To serve the dish

Warm four soup plates and place a spoonful of tomato in the centre of each plate. Pile the cucumber on top of the tomato to give height and dress six slices of scallop around the vegetables. Spoon the dressing over and around the fish and serve.

Loin of venison wrapped in a mousse of herbs and puff pastry served with a sauce of port and pickled walnut

SERVES 6

This can be served cut into slices or, especially for a dinner party, with the venison served in one piece.

1¹/₂lb (675g) loin of fallow deer, fully trimmed
2 garlic cloves
¹/₄ cinnamon stick
3 fl oz (75ml) olive oil
1 sprig fresh thyme
1 bay leaf
¹/₂oz (15g) thinly cut orange zest
1¹/₂lb (675g) venison bones
2oz (50g) each carrot, onion, celery
8 fl oz (225ml) red wine
1¹/₄pt (150ml) beef stock
3 fl oz (75ml) port
1 sprig thyme
1 juniper berry
redcurrant jelly
2oz (50g) pickled walnuts
arrowroot
5oz (150g) trimmed chicken breast
¹/₃oz each (8g) basil, chervil, tarragon
6oz (175g) double cream
5oz (150g) barding fat (in 1¹/₆in./2mm slices)
1lb (450g) puff pastry
1 egg

1. The day before (3 days if possible), ask the butcher to trim the loin down to the 'eye' of the meat, which should leave a strip of meat free of sinew and fat. Crush the garlic lightly and the cinnamon. Using a deep tray, roll the meat in the olive oil, lightly crushed garlic cloves, thyme, bay, zest and crushed

cinnamon stick. This will form the marinade for the meat, but will not dominate the flavour, as some red-wine marinades do. If a cheaper cut of meat is in use, then a marinade with some form of acid content will help tenderise the joint but in our case this should not be necessary if the meat is correctly hung prior to sale. (Cinnamon and orange were two of the spices used in the days before good refrigeration to discourage flies from attacking the game. But in our case I'm glad to say we need them just for their flavour benefits.)

2. Ensure the meat is well coated in the marinade, then cover with an oiled paper lid and refrigerate for at least a day.

3. To make the sauce of port and pickled walnuts, chop the venison bones into 1¼in. (3cm) sections and roast in a 400°F/200°C/Gas Mark 6 oven until browned.

4. Remove from the pan into a colander to drain, tip out any excess fat from the pan and brown the vegetables in the same pan on top of the stove.

5. Add the red wine and scrape the base of the pan to remove any sediment, then tip the red wine and vegetables into a stainless-steel pan.

6. Add the beef stock, drained bones and port and bring up to the simmer. Skim off any scum that forms and simmer the sauce very slowly for 40 minutes.

7. Add the thyme and crushed juniper berry and simmer for a further 10 minutes.

8. Strain the sauce through a muslin cloth into a clean pan and return to the heat.

9. Bring up to the simmer and add the redcurrant jelly, then allow the sauce to reduce until the correct depth of flavour is obtained (the time will depend upon the heat and stock you started off with).

10. Finish the sauce with the diced pickled walnuts and the few drops of the vinegar they are stored in, then thicken with the diluted arrowroot. The sauce may be made the day before and refrigerated. A little more of the vinegar may be required just before serving.

11. We now need to make a mousse to flavour and keep the meat moist. Dice up the chicken and purée in a food processor with the pickled herbs (no stalks) and a pinch of salt. The mixture should be smooth and green with a slight rubbery texture.

12. Using the pulse control on the machine (if you don't have a pulse control turn the machine on in 5-second bursts, checking after each mix), add the double cream in 4 or 5 batches and mix carefully until the mixture is smooth and pastel green, then season with more salt if needed and mill pepper. If the mousse is over-beaten in the machine the cream will turn to butter and ruin the mixture. All you can really do is either buy more chicken and start again or book yourselves in somewhere for dinner.

13. Refrigerate the mousse to firm it slightly.

14. Now heat a frying-pan large enough to take the venison until almost smoking. Roll the meat in the oil once more and place into the hot pan. Don't worry about the cinnamon and herbs sticking to the meat – it will all add extra flavour. Sear the meat on all sides then cook in the oven at 400°F/200°C/Gas Mark 6 for 8 minutes. Remove the meat on to a cooling wire to rest and cool.

15. Lay a sheet of grease-proof paper slightly longer than the meat on the table. Lay sheets of the sliced back fat on the paper large enough to roll the meat in. Spread the chicken mousse on the back fat $^1/_4$in. (6mm) deep. Place the cooled meat on the mousse, and use the paper to help roll the back fat over the meat, tucking in the ends. Roll the wrapped meat on to a tray lined with cling film and refrigerate to firm up the coating.

16. Roll out the puff pastry until $^1/_8$in. (3mm) thick, then cut a band deep enough to cover the meat generously but only four-fifths of the length. Using a trellis cutter rolled over the pastry, make a web of pastry and pull it open until it is long enough to enclose the venison.

17. Wrap the meat in the pastry, tucking the ends underneath the joint and sealing the joins with the beaten egg. Carefully transfer the joint to a baking sheet and glaze with beaten egg all over. The completed roll may now be refrigerated until needed.

18. After all our labours, at least the final stages are easy. Cook the finished venison in a 350–400°F/180–200°C/Gas Mark 4–6 oven for 20 minutes, then remove from the oven and allow to stand for 10 minutes. Warm the sauce and check the seasoning.

To serve the dish

Serve the meat cut in $^1/_2$in. ($1^1/_4$cm) slices with the sauce poured around, and garnish with boiled or roast celeriac. Roast parsnips also go well and make an excellent winter dish.

A gratin of summer fruits flavoured with Grand Marnier and elderflower sorbet

SERVES 4

This dessert makes use of local berry fruits and combines with the flavour of elderberry and the liqueur to produce a summer dessert with a hint of luxury. Out of season, try the sorbet with chilled melon and a little of the cordial poured over the melon prior to serving.

3 fl oz (85g) Sauternes wine
16 strawberries
24 raspberries
24 blueberries
$^1/_2$ mango
$^1/_2$ charantaise lemon
4 red plums
$^1/_2$ paw paw
$1^1/_2$ peaches
5 egg yolks (size 4)
$^4/_5$oz (20g) caster sugar
5 fl oz (160g) whipping cream
1oz (30g) caster sugar
1 cooked egg
$^4/_5$oz (20g) Grand Marnier
2oz (50g) escoffier paste (see recipe below)
4 scoops elderflower sorbet (see recipe below)
4 sprigs mint

1. Take a good bottle of Sauternes and place it in the fridge.
2. Hull and wash the strawberries, dry on kitchen paper and refrigerate.
3. Lightly wash the raspberries and blueberries, dry and refrigerate.
4. Peel the mango and cut into very thin slices the length of the fruit, then repeat this with the paw paw, removing the black seed from the centre of the fruit.
5. Place on a tray and refrigerate. Scoop out the melon with a melon-baller and season with a little of the cordial from the sorbet.
6. Slice the peaches but do not peel, then store with the other fruits.
7. Open the wine. Pour 85g (3oz) into a stainless-steel bowl with a curved base

165

and add the egg yolks and 20g of sugar. Pour yourself a good glass of the chilled wine, to refresh you for the next operation.

8. Place the bowl over a pan of hot but not boiling water (the bowl should not be in contact with the water but just above it). Beat the yolks with a whisk, lifting them as you whisk to incorporate air. After a few minutes the mixture will start to thicken. Once traces of the whisk are left in the mix it is cooked and can be removed from the heat. Whisk for two minutes more to cook the mixture, cover with cling film and put to one side. Finish the glass of wine.

9. Lightly whip the cream with the 30g (1oz) of sugar until traces of the whisk can just be seen, then carefully fold in the cooked egg and add the Grand Marnier. If the finished mixture is too thick, as can sometimes happen if either base is whipped too far, it may be thinned out with a little sugar syrup. The sauce should be thick enough to just coat the fruits when hot and allow some of the fruit to show through.

10. · Prepare four escoffier paste baskets (see recipe below) about 2in. (5cm) across to take a ball of the elderflower sorbet (see recipe below). This will insulate the sorbet from the hot plate.

Escoffier paste
5oz (150g) soft unsalted butter
8oz (225g) icing sugar
4oz (100g) golden syrup
4oz (100g) soft flour

1. Cream the butter and sugar together, add the syrup and fold in the flour. Rest for 24 hours in the fridge.
2. When required, mould into small balls, place on a baking tray and flatten with the palm of the hand.
3. Bake at 400°F/200°C/Gas Mark 6 until golden brown, remove from the oven and let cool slightly, then form as required.

Elderflower sorbet
15 fl oz (450ml) mineral water
8oz (240g) caster sugar
juice of $\frac{1}{2}$ lemon
6 strips of peeled lemon zest
6 strips of peeled orange zest
100ml elderflower cordial

1. The evening before you wish to freeze the sorbet, bring the water, sugar, lemon juice and zests up to the boil in a stainless-steel pan.

2. Allow to simmer for 5 minutes then tip the syrup into a bowl, cover with cling film and cool. When cool, place in the coldest part of the refrigerator.

3. The following day, strain the syrup to remove the zests and mix in the elderflower cordial. Freeze the mixture in an ice-cream machine until white and snowy. Store in a covered container in the freezer. If you don't have a machine, pour the mixture on to a shallow tray and place in the freezer. When the mix is three-quarters frozen quickly purée in a food processor and return to the freezer.

4. Do this twice more and the mix should be ready. Don't, however, allow the mix to melt during its time in the processor. Cooling the bowl of the machine in the freezer should help. If you are making ice-cream using this method, never melt and refreeze the mixture as this can lead to food poisoning. Always store the sorbets and ice-creams in covered containers as they will over a period of time be tainted by the freezer if left open to the air.

To serve the dish

Take a large plate and arrange the fruits, starting with the sliced fruit, in a haphazard pattern, making provision for the basket to fit in the centre. Next place on the berry fruits, starting with the largest, and the melon, filling in space with the smaller berries. (Other fruits can, of course, be used according to season.) Drizzle a little Grand Marnier over the fruit followed by the sauce. Don't be too generous with the sauce as it will spread during glazing – it's often a good idea to glaze a little of the sauce on some fruit beforehand to see how it will react. Quickly glaze the plate under a very hot grill and send to the table at once with a ball of the sorbet in its paste basket in the centre garnished with a sprig of mint.

Salad of winter fruits mulled in red wine accompanied by cinnamon ice-cream

SERVES 6

The best thing about this dish is that the whole operation can be done the day before. It can be used as a winter alternative to the gratin. It's a very robust dessert, with the mulled wine and spices leading to thoughts of Christmas.

12 fresh kumquats
$^{1}/_{2}$pt (300ml) sugar syrup
12 dried apricots
6 dried figs
12 dried apple rings
12 dried prunes (Argent)
12 dried peaches
6 dried pears
30 fl oz (900ml) red wine
15 fl oz (450ml) water
5 fl oz (150ml) dry sherry
5 fl oz (150ml) port
$^{1}/_{2}$ cinnamon stick
1 bay leaf
6oz (170g) redcurrant jelly
cinnamon ice-cream (see recipe below)

1. Bring the kumquats up to the simmer from cold in plain water, then drain and refresh in cold water. This operation will remove some of the bitterness from the fruit.
2. Now gently simmer the kumquats in the sugar syrup for 3 minutes and let cool in the juice.
3. Tie each of the dried fruits in a muslin bag and place in a glass or stainless container, allowing plenty of room for expansion. Bring the red wine and water to the boil and pour over the fruits. Allow to cool and refrigerate overnight.
4. The following day, drain off the liquid from the fruits and bring it up to the simmer in a stainless-steel pan. Add the sherry, port, cinnamon stick and bay leaf and simmer for 10 minutes. Skim off any scum as it rises to the surface.
5. Now our earlier labours with the muslin and string will pay off. Add each of the bags of fruit to the gently simmering liquid to cook. Exactly how long

168

each takes to cook will depend upon the quality of the fruits used, but expect the prunes and apple to cook quickly and the figs and pears to take the longest. As the fruits cook, they will exchange flavour with the sauce and become rich and mellow. However, be careful not to overcook and end up with a mush. Remove the fruits from the sauce as they are ready and allow them to cool in the bags.

6. Strain the sauce into a clean pan and add the redcurrant jelly in two halves, checking the flavour before putting the full amount in (this can also vary with the fruits used).

7. Store the fruits in their little bags covered with cling film (the wine will attack tinfoil). Make up the ice-cream and freeze in darole moulds and you are ready to go.

8. Warm the mulled fruits in the sauce – it should be thick enough to just coat the fruit, but if you are unhappy a little diluted arrowroot added to the sauce is quite permissible. Warm the kumquats in the cooking juices.

Cinnamon ice-cream
SERVES 4
1pt (600ml) double cream
1 vanilla pod
$1^{1}/_{4}$ cinnamon sticks
1oz (25g) Trimoline
5 egg yolks
3oz (75g) cinnamon sugar

1. Bring the cream to the boil, add the vanilla pod split in half along its length, then crush the cinnamon stick into the cream with your hands. Add the Trimoline and mix, cover the pan and leave to infuse for 15 minutes. (Trimoline is an invert sugar used as a stabiliser to prevent the ice-cream from becoming hard and granular. If you can't find it, don't worry, it won't affect the marvellous flavour of the cream – just add an extra egg yolk to help things out.)

2. We always store our cinnamon sticks in sugar, which provides us with a ready-made flavoured sugar for ice-cream and pastries and helps keep the sticks nice and dry. Again, if you haven't got any to hand, just use ordinary sugar and pack the leftover cinnamon in sugar ready for the next time. Take a large stainless bowl and beat the egg yolks and sugar together to lighten the mix. Return the cream to the simmer and pour one-third of the cream over the egg, whisking well. Pour this mixture back into the pan, stirring all the time with a wooden spoon.

3. Increase the heat and cook the cream until it starts to coat the back of the spoon and is too hot to put the tip of your very clean finger into. This can take a little practice, because if the cream is heated too much the egg will curdle and the mixture split. If this happens, don't lose heart – once the mixture is strained and cool, liquidise it for 30 seconds. It won't be quite as good but it's better than nothing.

4. If all is successful, strain the cream into a clean bowl and cover. Place on ice or in cold water to cool, then freeze as for the elderflower sorbet. Do heed the warning on refreezing (see p167) – this is a totally fresh product and has to be treated with respect.

To serve the dish

Dress the mulled fruits on a warm main-course place, arranging them around the edge to make space for the ice-cream. Pour the sauce over the fruits and place the kumquats around to give colour. Turn the cinnamon ice-cream out on to the centre of the plate and garnish with fresh mint. As your guests eat the dessert, the ice-cream will melt slightly, forming a second sauce.

CHAPTER TEN

FERRIER RICHARDSON

Fish soup with saffron and Gruyère soufflé has evolved from the traditional soup served with roué and Parmesan. All the ingredients normally found in the roué were put in the soufflé. It's quite stunning to serve because the heat of the soup helps to keep the soufflé up. There are almost limitless varieties – smoked haddock with Orkney cheddar, onion with Gruyère.

Ideas sometimes hit me and sometimes they evolve more slowly. Sometimes dishes can take a year or so to come to their final form; others I'm happy with right away.

Puddings are very important to me. The thing about a dessert is that it should be a showstopper, it's the climax you've been building up to. I developed a Grand Dessert when I was at the Buttery, and it's as big a seller now as it was 12 years ago.

My interest in Japanese cooking stems from the time I spent in Ma Cuisine in London. For the staff lunch, we might have proper Japanese-style food. It would start off being served on a plate, and then the black lacquer tray was being used. By the time I opened October restaurant the food had evolved. I'm more interested in Japanese and Chinese food.

FERRIER RICHARDSON has just opened a new restaurant in Glasgow called Yes!. Prior to that he was executive chef at the Glasgow Hilton. Previously he had been head chef at the Rogano and the Buttery in Glasgow before opening his own restaurant in Bearsden called October. As manager of the Scottish Culinary Olympic Team, he has collected gold medals in competitions in Frankfurt and Singapore. He is a founder member of the Scottish Chefs Association and sits on its Advisory Board.

Fish soup with saffron-and-Gruyère soufflé

SERVES 6

This is a very simple dish to make, but quite stunning to serve. If you feel you're not up to making the soufflé, then you will find the soup itself is equally satisfying.

6 cloves garlic
9oz (250g) mixed vegetables, including fennel, carrot, onion, celery and leeks
6oz (175g) salmon fillet
4oz (100–125g) haddock fillet
2 tbsp virgin olive oil
1oz (25g) butter
5 fl oz (150ml) white wine
5 fl oz (150ml) red wine
$3^1/_2$ fl oz (90ml) tomato purée
4oz (100–125g) canned tomatoes
1 tbsp fennel seeds
1 tbsp tarragon
1 tbsp thyme
1 tbsp parsley
3 bay leaves
1 tsp cayenne pepper
2 fl oz (60ml) brandy
$1^1/_2$pt (900ml) good-quality fish stock
1 tbsp saffron threads
9 large basil leaves
saffron-and-Gruyère soufflé (see recipe below)

1. Crush garlic and finely dice the vegetables.
2. Chop tarragon, thyme, parsley and canned tomatoes.
3. Cut salmon and haddock into small pieces.
4. Heat oil and butter in saucepan and cook garlic and diced vegetables over a medium heat for 5–10 minutes or until golden brown.
5. Add white wine and deglaze pan.
6. Add red wine, tomato purée, chopped tomato, fennel seeds, tarragon, thyme, parsley, bay leaves and cayenne. Season to taste with salt and fresh-ground black pepper.
7. Add brandy and salmon and haddock and cook over a low-to-medium heat

172

for 5 minutes.

8. Add the stock and simmer for 25 minutes.
9. Add the saffron and basil and cook for 5 more minutes.
10. Process the soup in batches in a food processor until smooth and then pass through sieve. Season to taste with salt and black pepper.
11. Make saffron-and-Gruyère soufflé (see recipe below).
12. Pour the soup two-thirds of the way up 6 oven-proof soup bowls.
13. Top with soufflé mixture.
14. Bake at 425°F/220°C/Gas Mark 7 for 12 minutes or until soufflés are well puffed and golden. Serve immediately.

Saffron-and-Gruyère soufflé

4oz (125g) Gruyère
1oz (30g) butter
1oz (30g) flour
400ml milk
1 tsp saffron threads
4 egg yolks
3 tbsp freshly snipped chives
6 egg whites

1. Grate Gruyère.
2. Melt butter in a saucepan and stir in the flour. Cook over a low heat for 3 minutes.
3. Remove pan from heat and gradually blend in milk with a wooden spoon.
4. Return to heat and cook over a medium heat, stirring constantly until sauce boils and thickens.
5. Add saffron and season to taste with salt and pepper and set aside to cool.
6. Beat egg yolks into cooled mixture. Stir in Gruyère and chives. Whisk egg whites with a pinch of salt until soft peaks form. Gently fold into the sauce.

Breast of pheasant with a tarragon mousseline and red-wine essence

SERVES 4

This is a rich-flavoured game dish enhanced by the mousseline and sauce. It is relatively sinmple to prepare, but very rewarding on the table.

2oz (50g) tarragon leaves
2 pheasants
$^1/_2$ egg white
1 egg yolk
$^1/_3$pt (200ml) cream
4 large square crepinette (pig's caul)
seasoning
1 carrot
$^1/_2$ turnip
1 courgette
12 shallots
1 potato
$^1/_2$ savoy cabbage
mirepoix of carrot, onion and celery
1pt (600ml) water
arrowroot

1. Chop 1oz (25g) tarragon leaves. Put the rest to one side for the garnish at the end.
2. Remove breasts and thighs from pheasants. Set carcases to one side.
3. Seal the breasts and leave to cool.
4. Process thighs in food processor. When finely processed, add egg white and then cream to mousse stage.
5. Add chopped tarragon and season.
6. Spread the mousseline over the pheasant breast and cover with crepinette.
7. Roast the pheasant breasts in the oven at 475°F/240°C/Gas Mark 9 for 8 minutes.
8. Shape carrot, turnip and courgette. Cool until crisp.
9. Roast shallots.
10. Prepare potato and cabbage galettes. Shred potato and cabbage finely. Add egg yolk and seasoning. Starting with potato and finishing with potato, interleave

layers of potato and cabbage. Cook in cutters to form 4in. (10cm) discs 3 minutes either side on a medium gas until golden brown.

11. Roast the pheasant carcases and the mirepoix on 425°F/200°C/Gas Mark 7 for 30 minutes until brown.

12. Deglaze with red wine and add 1pt (600ml) water. Reduce to $^1/_2$pt (300ml). Strain with fine sieve and thicken slightly with a touch of arrowroot.

To serve the dish

Place the pheasant on top of the galette. Surround with vegetables and pour round the sauce. Garnish with a sprig of fresh tarragon.

Seafood casserole with leek and ginger essence

SERVES 4

Scotland is so rich in seafood that it is easy to find the ingredients for a very satisfying seafood casserole. The leek and ginger essence add an extra element of flavour.

8oz (225g) leeks
1oz (25g) fresh ginger
1 tbsp chives
seasoning
$^{1}/_{4}$pt (150ml) white wine
$^{1}/_{8}$pt (75ml) fish stock
4oz (100–125g) salmon
4oz (100–125g) monkfish
4oz (100–125g) scallops
4oz (100–125g) mussel meat
4oz (100–125g) prawns
$^{3}/_{4}$pt (450ml) double cream

1. Cut the leeks into matchstick strips to make a julienne. Steam the leeks.
2. Peel and slice the fresh ginger.
3. Finely chop the chives until you have one tbsp.
4. Place white wine in a pan and cook until it has reduced by half.
5. Add fish stock and bring to the boil. Reduce to a simmer.
6. Add seafood and blanch (remove when half-cooked), doing salmon and monkfish first, then the scallops, mussels and prawns. Cook for about two minutes, until translucent.
7. Add the ginger to the liquid and then the double cream. Cook until this sauce coats the back of the spoon.
8. Strain into another pot, removing the ginger.
9. Add the seafood and gently warm.

To serve the dish
Place the steamed leeks in the centre of a warm, flat soup plate. Add chopped chives to the seafood and ginger essence and spoon round the steamed leeks.

Supreme of salmon with potato scales and a spaghetti of vegetables with a dill-butter sauce

SERVES 4

The various elements involved in this dish give it an attractive appearance as well as a good mixture of textures and flavour.

2lb (1kg) potatoes
4oz (100–125g) leeks (whites)
4oz (100–125g) courgettes
4oz (100–125g) turnip
4oz (100–125g) carrot
4 x 6oz (175g) fillets of salmon
4oz (100–125g) clarified butter
$^1/_4$pt (150ml) white wine
$^1/_8$pt (75ml) fish stock
$^1/_2$lb (225g) unsalted butter
$^1/_4$pt (150ml) double cream
seasoning
2 tbsp chopped dill
$^1/_2$ lemon

1. Cut the potatoes into $1^1/_2$in. (4cm) diameter and $^1/_8$in. (3mm) thick slices. You need 48 slices.
2. Cut the leeks, courgettes, turnip and carrot into thin slices like spaghetti.
3. Place salmon on a baking tray.
4. Dip potatoes in clarified butter and lay them on salmon 3 abreast and 4 deep.
5. Season the salmon, cook in oven at 425°F/220°C/Gas Mark 7 for 8 minutes.
6. Prepare vegetables, blanch and keep warm.
7. To make the dill-butter sauce, place white wine in a pan and reduce by half. Add the fish stock and bring to the boil. Add the butter in pieces using a whisk. This should result in an emulsion. Finish by adding the cream.
8. Check the seasoning. Add the dill and a squeeze of lemon at last moment.

To serve the dish
Place the vegetable spaghetti on plate in a circle with roast salmon and surround with dill-butter sauce.

Teriyaki beef

SERVES 4

This is a very quick and interesting dish. The flavours are excellent with plenty of contrast. In Japan it is traditional to serve a bowl of soup with this dish, but I find that the beef and rice is more than enough for a main course.

1¹/₂lb (675g) fillet beef
¹/₃pt (200ml) teriyaki sauce
8oz (225g) Japanese rice
1 tsp wasabi powder
3 tbsp sesame oil
2oz pickled ginger
seasoning

1. Cut beef into 2in. x ¹/₂in. (5cm x 1cm) strips and marinade in teriyaki sauce for 1 hour.
2. Cook rice.
3. Prepare wasabi powder (instructions on packet).
4. Drain beef from marinade and keep marinade to the side.
5. Heat a wok or frying-pan with sesame oil.
6. Place beef in wok and fry till rare.
7. Add half of the marinade and cook for 1 minute.

To serve the dish
Place the rice in a large bowl. Place the beef in a small bowl topped with the pickled ginger. Place the wasabi in a small bowl.

Honey, Glayva and almond delice

SERVES 4

This is one of my favourite desserts. It is quite straightforward to prepare, and the contrast between the Glayva and the almonds makes it quite refreshing.

1pt (600ml) milk
8 egg yolks
6oz (175g) sugar
1 tsp almond essence
3 leaves gelatine
2 fl oz (50ml) Glayva
3 fl oz (75ml) honey
16 fl oz (475ml) double cream
1 genoise sponge (to line bottom of 9in. x 1^1/$_2$in. (23 x 4cm) cake tin)

1. Make a crème anglaise with milk, egg yolks, sugar and almond essence. Cool to room temperature.
2. Soak gelatine in cold water for 15 minutes, then drain.
3. Warm Glayva and honey and stir in gelatine.
4. Whip cream until it reaches the ribbon stage.
5. Stir Glayva mixture into cooked crème anglaise, then fold into cream.
6. Place the mixture in ring on top of genoise sponge soaked with Glayva syrup and place in fridge to set.

To serve the dish
Remove the ring and cut into portions using a knife that has been dipped in hot water. Garnish with sauce anglaise and seasonal fruits.

Strawberry-and-rhubarb parfait

This is another very simple pudding. The contrast in flavours between the strawberry and rhubarb gives the dish an extra lift.

8oz (225g) rhubarb
8oz (225g) strawberries
4oz (100–125g) granulated sugar
2 large sprigs of mint
2 tbsp dessert wine
2 tbsp sugar
2 tbsp sugar syrup
3 eggs
$^1/_3$pt (200ml) double cream

1. Peel rhubarb and place into a pot the peeled rhubarb, strawberries, sugar and mint with the dessert wine.
2. Bring to the boil and simmer for 10 minutes until fruit is soft.
3. Blend in a food processor until a purée forms and sieve and leave to cool.
4. Whisk sugar, sugar syrup and egg yolks over a bain-marie until light and frothy (ribbon stage). Remove from heat.
5. Whisk egg whites and double cream to soft peaks.
6. Add purée to cooled egg yolks, gently fold in cream then the egg whites.
7. Place in a terrine or individual moulds and freeze.

To serve the dish
Turn out or slice and place on plates. Serve with a fruit coulis or sauce anglaise or fine dice of strawberries and mint.

CHAPTER ELEVEN

ANDREW RADFORD

I ASSOCIATE widgeon, a type of duck, with an inspirational time for me. It goes back about a decade to when I was at Cromlix House in Perthshire and just thinking about becoming a cook. Then widgeon was served only rarely. I would imagine that for every one widgeon dish we served we would serve about 5–6 teal and about 20 mallard. Nowadays, the proportions are not much different – about 6 widgeon to every 50 mallard. But I find cooking and eating widgeon very enjoyable. It has a very distinctive flavour and it's a beautiful bird. My *widgeon, roast roots and wild mushrooms served with potato stacks* is a very Scottish dish. It's a winter dish and incorporates so many of Scotland's great vegetables. It also proves that good food need not be expensive. Widgeon is about one-third the price of mallard and, of course, the vegetables are not particularly expensive. The cooked vegetables have a good caramel colour and the browned sweetness goes very well with the widgeon. The vegetables add a good variety of colour. You could do the vegetables on their own as a casserole, and the dish can be made with all the vegetables or larger quantities of just one or a few of the vegetables. To get hold of the widgeon, you will need to go to a good butcher or a game dealer.

I've always enjoyed white fish, although cod has always, for some reason, been regarded as the poor man's fish. But a good piece of cod, cooked lightly, is a wonderful flaky and moist fish. My *cod with leek and salsa crumb* combines traditional and modern ideas. Leek is one of my favourite vegetables because it goes with anything, but it is particularly good with fish. The salsa gives the dish a bit more spice, and the crumb gives the moist fish and the salsa more bite. The crumb is used a bit like a crumble. I've actually used the crumb idea with a dish of langoustine and pesto and called it langoustine crumble.

Parmesan tart of langoustine and spinach with olive oil and basil is a savoury version of shortbread tart. It's a great base for any filling. I use the tart idea also as a vegetable dish with mushrooms and spinach. The dish is simple and clean with different textures of crunch and softness. There is a contrast in the bite, with the softness cutting against the tart. The tart is a foil against the lightly and perfectly cooked langoustine. The dish is put together so late that the tart is still crisp and crunchy. Spinach and fish traditionally go well together. Young spinach needs very little cooking – the warmth of whatever it is laid against is almost as much as it needs. This is one of our popular dishes and we serve it both as a main course and in smaller quantities as a starter.

ANDREW RADFORD opened The Atrium in Edinburgh with his wife, Lisa, last year and it has been a success from the start, winning many awards along the way. Andrew already had a strong following in Edinburgh, where he had gained a reputation for his cooking at Waterloo Place and Handsels, but his culinary education really began as chef on the Royal Scotsman train. Andrew is a founder member of the Scottish Chefs Association and serves on its Advisory Board.

Cod with leek and salsa crumb

SERVES 4

You can use haddock with this dish instead of cod. If you reduce the fish portion size and leave out the potatoes, you could serve it as a starter.

6oz (175g) salsa (see recipe below)
butter sauce (see recipe below)
4oz (100–125g) brioche or bread
1oz (25g) chive
1lb (450g) leek
8oz (225g) new potato
4 x 6oz (175g) cod portions
olive oil
salt and pepper for seasoning

1. Make the salsa (see recipe below). This can be done the night before.
2. Make the butter sauce (see recipe below). When ready, this can stand for about 30 minutes beside the stove.
3. Using a processor, turn the bread or brioche into fine crumbs.
4. Chop the chives.
5. Cut the leek into small squares.
6. Cut the potatoes into slices and cook until almost at eating consistency.
7. Place the cod on a baking tray. Brush with olive oil and season with salt and pepper.
8. Grill the cod under a high heat for 3–4 minutes.
9. While the cod is grilling, very quickly at a very high heat pan-fry the potato slices and the squares of leek in a little olive oil for 1 minute. This is almost like a quick stir-fry.
10. Remove the cod and spoon a little salsa on each cod portion. Sprinkle with the brioche or bread crumbs.
11. Place the cod back under the grill to brown.

Salsa

4 large plum tomatoes
1 red chilli
2 spring onions
$1/2$ red pepper
1 clove garlic (optional)
1 tbsp white-wine vinegar (or juice of lemon)
1 tbsp tomato purée (optional)
1 tbsp coriander

1. Roughly chop the tomatoes, chilli, spring onion, red pepper and garlic.
2. Place these ingredients in a food processor with vinegar (or lemon juice), tomato purée (if used) and the coriander. Blitz for a few seconds until a rough mix is achieved.

Butter sauce

1 shallot
3 fl oz (75ml) white wine
2 fl oz (50ml) white-wine vinegar
basil/tarragon/parsley stalks
4oz (100–125g) double cream
4oz (100–125g) butter

1. Peel and roughly chop the shallot.
2. Place the wine, wine vinegar, shallot and stalks into a thick-bottomed pan and cook until reduced by half.
3. Add the double cream and reduce again (taking care not to boil over) until you have a thick, syrupy sauce.
4. Take the butter straight from the fridge, cut into small cubes and whisk into the reduced sauce.
5. Strain and store in a small pan close to the heat.

To serve the dish

Spoon some of the potato and leek mixture on to the centre of each plate. Place a cod portion with salsa topping on the top of the potato and leek mixture. Pour some butter sauce alongside. Sprinkle with the chopped chive and serve.

Grilled halibut with basil pesto, spinach and rocket

SERVES 4

This dish makes a delicious meal in itself, but by adding a potato stack — as used in the Widgeon dish (see page 190) — it can be turned into an even more substantial main course.

1oz (25g) shallot
8oz (225g) baby spinach leaves
4oz (100–125g) rocket leaves
2oz (50g) basil leaves
salt and pepper for seasoning
4 fl oz (100–125ml) pesto (see recipe below)
3 fl oz (75ml) pesto dressing (see recipe below)
olive oil
4 x 6oz (175g) halibut fillets
1oz (25g) parsley, chopped

1. Finely chop the shallot and the parsley.
2. In a large bowl mix together the spinach, rocket and basil leaves with a little salt.
3. Make the pesto (see recipe below).
4. Make the pesto dressing (see recipe below).
5. Place the halibut fillets on a baking tray and brush with olive oil and season with salt and pepper.
6. Place the halibut tray under a high grill and cook for 3–4 minutes (depending on the thickness of the halibut fillets, but when cooked it should remain moist to the touch).
7. Meanwhile, sprinkle the chopped shallot and a little of the pesto dressing on to the mixture of spinach, rocket and basil leaves.
8. When the halibut is cooked, sprinkle liberally with the chopped parsley.

Pesto

4oz (100–125g) basil
2 cloves garlic
4oz (100–125g) pine nuts
2oz (50g) Reggiano Parmesan
2oz (50g) olive oil

1. Put the basil, garlic, pine nuts and Parmesan into a blender and blitz.
2. Pour in olive oil. The result should be a coarse paste.

Pesto dressing

1 fl oz (25ml) pesto
2 fl oz (25ml) olive oil

Add the pesto to the olive oil.

To serve the dish

Place the dressed mixture of spinach, rocket and basil leaves on each plate. Place one halibut fillet on top of the leaves. Place a teaspoon of pesto on top of each fillet. Drizzle a little more pesto dressing around the leaves.

Grilled salmon with red pepper, plum tomato and courgette in a fine-herb olive oil

SERVES 4

Scottish and Mediterranean cooking meet! This is an ideally simple dish in which wonderful ratatouille-type ingredients come together in a chunky style. It's a great dish for summer lunch.

2 red peppers
4 courgettes
4 plum tomatoes
4oz (100–125g) in total mixture of basil, dill, flat parsley, coriander, curly parsley and chive
4 x 6oz (175g) salmon (cut from the boned fillet)
olive oil
salt and pepper for seasoning

1. Cut the red peppers in half and de-seed.
2. Cut the courgettes and plum tomatoes in half lengthways.
3. Wash, pick and finely chop the basil, dill, flat parsley, coriander, curly parsley and chive.
4. Place the four halves of red pepper skin-side up under a hot grill until the skin begins to brown and blister.
5. Place the red peppers in a bowl and cover with cling film. (The hot pepper will create steam, which will lift the skin from the pepper flesh.)
6. After 5 minutes, remove the cling film, then carefully peel off the skin. (Any skin which still proves stubborn can be removed with a sharp knife, but try to keep the pepper halves intact.)
7. Place the salmon, the pepper halves, courgette and tomato on a baking tray and brush with olive oil. Season with salt and pepper.
8. Grill for approx. 4 minutes until the salmon is cooked. (The vegetables should also be ready in this time.)

To serve the dish

Warm your plates. Arrange the vegetables in a haphazard overlapping manner. Arrange the salmon on top. Drizzle with olive oil and sprinkle with the finely chopped herbs.

Parmesan tart of langoustine and spinach with olive oil and basil

SERVES 4

This is an ideal dish for cooking at home. All the work for the Parmesan tarts is done in advance (you need to leave a couple of hours for letting the dough mix rest and for subsequent refrigeration). But the actual cooking of the langoustine and spinach filling takes just minutes.

4 Parmesan tarts (see recipe below)
1¹/₂lb (675g) langoustine tails
2oz (50g) parsley
2oz (50g) shallot
1oz (25g) basil leaves
1oz (25g) garlic
1lb (450g) small spinach leaves
olive oil

1. Make the Parmesan tarts (see recipe below), allowing a couple of hours for this stage.
2. Peel the langoustine tails.
3. Finely chop the parsley and shallot.
4. Chop the garlic.
5. Wash and dry the spinach leaves.
6. Pan-fry the langoustine tails quickly with the garlic and shallots. After 2–3 minutes stir in the spinach.
7. Divide this mixture between the cooked tarts.

Parmesan tarts
4oz (100–125g) Parmesan cheese
2¹/₂oz (65g) plain flour
2oz (50g) butter
salt
cayenne pepper (optional)
4 individual tart moulds

1. Grate the Parmesan cheese.
2. Mix the flour and butter together with a pinch of salt.

3. Fold in the Parmesan and cayenne (if used) and mix until you have a soft dough.
4. Allow to rest for 1 hour (note: this mix will keep for up to a week in the fridge).
5. Butter the tart moulds, then line with the pastry.
6. Refrigerate for 1 hour.
7. Bake the tarts in a moderate oven until golden brown.

To serve the dish

Place each tart on a plate. Dribble with olive oil and sprinkle with the finely chopped parsley and basil leaves.

Widgeon, roast roots and wild mushroom served with potato stacks

SERVES 4

This is what I see as a typical Scottish dish – rich and full of flavour, but really very simple to prepare. Served with potato stacks, it makes an ample meal. Widgeon is a type of duck, slightly larger than teal, which feeds on sea fish. It is ideal for cooking because of its flavour and because it cooks so quickly. If widgeon is not available, you can use pigeon, teal or mallard.

4 widgeons
1pt (600ml) brown stock (see recipe below)
4–6oz (100–175g) wild mushrooms
1 tsp redcurrant jelly
8oz (225g) new potatoes
6oz (175g) carrot
4oz (100–125g) parsnip
4oz (100–125g) celeriac
4oz (100–125g) swede
4 medium-sized shallots
6oz (175g) leek
potato stack (see recipe below)
olive oil
salt and pepper for seasoning
2oz (50g) parsley

1. Remove the breasts from the widgeon and place in a little olive oil, then cover with cling film. (This can be done up to 1 week before cooking. It improves the flavour and makes the flesh more tender.) Hold on to the carcases as an ingredient for the brown stock or make use of them separately for a game stock for another dish.
2. Make the brown stock (see recipe below). You need to allow about 3 hours to make the stock, but it can be done the day (or several days) before.
3. Clean and trim the wild mushrooms. Retain the stalks.
4. Place 1pt of the reduced brown stock sauce in a thick-bottomed pan, along with the mushroom stalks and the redcurrant jelly. Reduce by half over a low heat until the sauce has thickened slightly.
5. Slice the new potatoes skin-on into $^{1}/_{4}$in. (6mm) rings and par cook.

6. Dice the carrot, parsnip, celeriac, swede, shallot and leek.
7. Make the potato stacks (see recipe below) and put into oven.
8. Place the diced carrot, swede and shallot, along with the sliced part-cooked potato, into a roasting tray with a little olive oil and salt and pepper. Roast in a high oven at 325°F/170°C/Gas Mark 3 for 5 minutes.
9. Meanwhile, pan-fry the widgeon breasts at a fairly high heat for 1 minute each side and season with salt and pepper.
10. Remove the widgeon breasts from the heat. Cover with a lid to retain the heat and let the breasts rest. The pan will continue to cook the meat but not with direct heat so the breasts will not toughen. Also, by this point the heat will not have reached the middle of the breasts, but with the lid on blood will be drawn from the middle to the outer parts of the breast so that when you slice the breasts you will get an even pinkness.
11. Add the leek to the roast vegetables and return to the oven for a further 3–4 minutes.
12. Meanwhile, reheat the brown stock sauce.
13. Carve each breast into 2 or 3 slices.
14. Remove the vegetables from the oven. Add the mushrooms and quickly toss together.

Brown stock
2lb (900g) beef/lamb bones or 1lb (450g) beef/lamb bones and the
    4 widgeon carcases
2 carrots
2 sticks celery
parsley stalks and leek trimmings
olive oil
1 bottle red wine
6pt ($3^1/_2$l) water

1. Brown the bones in the oven at 400°F/200°C/Gas Mark 6 for 40 minutes.
2. Wash and chop the vegetables.
3. Brown the vegetables in a little olive oil in your largest pan.
4. Add the red wine and water. Bring to the boil and skim.
5. Add the bones and simmer for 2–3 hours.
6. Strain the stock. Return to the heat and reduce by half. (This will give you 3pt of stock, which is too much for the dish. Retain only 1pt of this reduced sauce. You can refrigerate or freeze the leftover 2pt in smaller quantities.)

Potato stacks

2 baking potatoes
$^1/_4$pt olive oil
salt and pepper for seasoning

1. Slice the potatoes very thin (about $^1/_8$in.).
2. Place the slices in a bowl with the olive oil and a pinch of salt and pepper and mix together.
3. Re-stack the slices into 4 piles.
4. Roast the stacks at 400°F/200°C/Gas Mark 6 for approx. 20–30 minutes until golden.
   (Note: Potato stacks can easily stand on their own or be used with a lot of other dishes. You can add flavour to the dish by using other herbs, such as chilli, ground black pepper, juniper, coriander, tarragon, dill or parsley.)

To serve the dish

Spoon a pile of roast vegetables on to the centre of each plate. On top place the sliced widgeon breast. Divide up the sauce and pour equal amounts over each breast. Sprinkle with the chopped parsley. Serve the potato stacks at the side of the plate.

Andrew Radford
WIDGEON, ROAST ROOTS AND WILD MUSHROOM SERVED WITH POTATO STACKS

FERRIER RICHARDSON

ANDREW RADFORD

BETTY ALLEN

Ferrier Richardson
TERIYAKI BEEF

Betty Allen

FILLET OF HALIBUT ON LENTIL DU PUY WITH SHIITAKI MUSHROOMS AND A TARRAGON SAUCE

Amaretto ice-cream with almond biscuits

SERVES 4

This is a simple ice-cream recipe for people who think making ice-cream is difficult. You don't have to use Amaretto, you can use any liqueur – Tia Maria, Drambuie, Cointreau – as long as the liqueur is well-incorporated into the ice-cream. Equally, for the biscuits, you can use any kind of nuts – pecan, Brazil, pistachio, etc.

almond biscuits (see recipe below)
6 eggs (any size)
6oz (175g) vanilla sugar
1pt (600ml) cream
$^1/_2$pt (300ml) Amaretto

1. Make the almond biscuits (see recipe below). This can be done 3–4 days in advance.
2. Put a pan of water on to boil.
3. Place the eggs and sugar in a bowl and whisk together over the water, which should be simmering, until a thick custard is formed.
4. Allow to cool.
5. Whisk the cream until a similar consistency is reached.
6. Pour the cream into the custard and mix together.
7. Add Amaretto and freeze until firm, but not too hard.

Almond biscuits
4oz (100–125g) almonds
4oz (100–125g) plain flour
4oz (100–125g) butter
4oz (100–125g) caster sugar

1. Grind the nuts until rough.
2. Mix all the ingredients together.
3. Roll the whole batch into a fat cylinder about 3in. ($^1/_2$cm) in diameter.
4. Refrigerate your fat cyclinder until hard.
5. Remove the cylinder from the fridge and slice into $^1/_4$in. ($^1/_2$cm) slices.

193

6. Place the slices on a baking tray and bake in a high oven at 325°F/170°C/Gas Mark 3 for 10–12 minutes until golden. Allow to cool.
7. Lift off tray and serve immediately (if making in advance, keep the fat cylinder in the fridge for 3–4 days and remove, slice and bake on the night).

To serve the dish
Serve the ice-cream with the almond biscuits.

CHAPTER TWELVE

BETTY ALLEN

ERIC and I spent our honeymoon in Argyll and had the idea then that it would be wonderful to live and work in such a lovely environment. Some years later, our dream came true, and we bought the Airds Hotel in 1978.

Two of the highlights have been the award of Chef Laureate from the British Academy of Gastronomes in 1987 and a star from Michelin in 1991. We are delighted too that our son and daughter-in-law, Graeme and Anne, now play a major role in running the hotel.

The recipe for *walnut fudge* tart was given to me by my mother, who cooked for a family in Edinburgh before she was married. When I took over the cooking here, I was searching around for ideas and remembered how much we liked it as children. It has been so popular that it has appeared on the menu here for 17 years.

Terrine of chicken livers

SERVES 4

This is an unusual kind of terrine, but the main ingredient is cheap and the end result is delicious.

1lb (450g) chicken livers
2 tbsp port
10oz (275g) goose or duck fat
8 egg yolks
5oz (150g) unsalted butter
$^3/_4$pt (450ml) double cream
$^1/_2$ garlic clove, finely chopped
1 pinch cayenne pepper
1 pinch grated nutmeg
2 fl oz (50ml) cognac
1 tsp salt

1. Clean the livers and marinate in the port for 24 hours.
2. Put them in a sieve and rinse, then leave to drain.
3. Melt the fats, put everything together and process.
4. Taste and re-season if necessary.
5. Put through a sieve and into a jug.
6. Line the bottom of a non-stick loaf tin (8in. x 4in./20cm x 10cm) with bakewell paper and bring it up over the two short ends with an overhang of about two inches.
7. Pour the mixture into the tin and cover loosely with foil.
8. Place in a deep tray which contains enough water to come halfway up the sides of the tin and bake in a preheated oven at 375°F/190°C/Gas Mark 5, until only just firm in the centre, for about 1 hour and 15 minutes.
9. Allow to cool and then cover with cling film and refrigerate.

To serve the dish
Turn the terrine on to a board and cut into slices using a warm knife. Serve with buttered toast.

Fillet of halibut on lentil du Puy with Shiitaki mushrooms and a tarragon sauce

SERVES 4

Halibut is one of my favourite kinds of fish. The mushrooms and lentils add texture and flavour.

6oz (175g) lentils (preferably Puy)
$^1/_2$ an onion, peeled
1 bay leaf
1pt (600ml) chicken stock
salt and freshly ground pepper
2 tbsp chopped coriander
4 x 6oz (175g) halibut or cod fillets
a little plain flour
salt and pepper
butter
12 shiitaki mushrooms (stalks removed)

1. Wash the lentils, place in a pan with the onion and bay leaf and cover with chicken stock.
2. Simmer until cooked (about 25 minutes), adding extra liquid if required. Season and add coriander just before serving.
3. Lightly coat the fish in the seasoned flour and fry in butter. Keep warm.
4. At the same time fry the mushrooms and season.

To serve the dish
Divide the lentils between four plates, sit the fish on the lentils and arrange the mushrooms on top of the fish. Pour the sauce around.

Roast stuffed saddle of lamb

SERVES 4

There could hardly be a simpler dish than this, and yet it is full of flavour.

1 x 4lb (1.8kg) short saddle of lamb
1oz (25g) butter
1 shallot
$^{1}/_{2}$ clove of garlic
6oz (175g) chicken breasts
1 small egg
2 tbsp double cream
parsley, chives and tarragon
salt and freshly ground pepper

1. Remove the paper-thin skin from the outside of the saddle, bone out completely (this can be done by your butcher) and keep the two fillets. Remove all the excess fat from the flaps so they are as thin and as even as possible. Try not to make any holes.
2. Melt the butter and gently sauté the finely chopped shallot and garlic until soft. Drain off any liquid, transfer to a plate and cool in the fridge.
3. Finely mince or process the chicken. Remove from the processor and put the chicken into a bowl set in a larger bowl of ice. Using an electric hand whisk at low setting, beat in the lightly beaten egg, cream, shallots and garlic.
4. Add the herbs, taste and season.
5. Sprinkle the meat with a little salt and pepper and lay the mixture along the centre (you may not need it all).
6. Place one of the fillets on top and roll up.
7. Use some tinfoil at each end to keep the stuffing in place and tie with string at regular intervals.
8. Roast the meat in a preheated oven at 425°F/220°C/Gas Mark 6 for 30–45 minutes, depending on thickness. It is best served fairly pink.
9. Remove from the oven, cover and leave to rest in a warm place for 15 minutes.

To serve the dish
Carve in thick slices to serve.

Mousse of mango with walnut shortbread

SERVES 10

I have found this to be an interesting combination, full of contrast in flavour and texture. You can, of course, do the shortbread on its own.

3 dessertspoons of water
3 tsp lemon juice
1 rounded dessertspoon of powdered gelatine
6 mangoes
2 tbsp rum
$2^{1}/_{2}$oz (65g) soft brown sugar
$1^{1}/_{2}$ tsp ground ginger
$^{1}/_{2}$ pt (300ml) double cream
walnut shortbread (see recipe below)

1. Put the water and lemon juice in a small, thick-bottomed pan, sprinkle on the gelatine and dissolve slowly over a very low heat.
2. Purée mangoes, measure $^{3}/_{4}$pt (450ml) and return to the processor. Reserve the remainder of the purée.
3. Add the rum, sugar and ginger to the purée and pour in the gelatine mixture through a sieve.
4. Purée until all is smooth.
5. Lightly whip the cream and fold the mango mixture into the cream.
6. Pour into a jug and fill lightly buttered ramekins.
7. Refrigerate for 6 hours or until lightly set.
8. Pour the purée on to the plates, turn out the mousse and set on the purée.

Walnut shortbread
7oz (200g) plain flour, sieved
4oz (100–125g) finely chopped walnuts
8oz (225g) unsalted butter, softened
4oz (100–125g) icing sugar
2 small egg yolks
$^{1}/_{4}$ tsp vanilla essence

1. Put all ingredients into the processor and process until everything comes together and forms a ball.

2. Wrap in cling film and chill for about 4 hours.
3. Remove from fridge and allow to come up to room temperature.
4. Then roll out thinly, cut into heart shapes and place on a lightly buttered baking sheet.
5. Paint with lightly whipped egg white and dust with sieved icing sugar.
6. Bake in oven preheated to 425°F/220°C/Gas Mark 7 for 5–10 minutes.
7. Cool on a wire rack.

To serve the dish
Serve the mousse with the shortbread biscuits.

Walnut fudge tart

I am a great fan of walnut, and this pudding is an excellent way to savour it.

3oz (75g) butter
3oz (75g) lard
12oz (350g) plain flour
17oz (475g) granulated sugar
1$\frac{1}{2}$ small eggs
4$\frac{1}{2}$ fl oz (140 ml) water
12 fl oz (350ml) double cream
12oz (350g) chopped walnuts

1. Make the pastry by rubbing the butter and lard into the flour until it resembles fine breadcrumbs.
2. Mix in 5oz (150g) of the sugar and bind together with the eggs.
3. Knead to a smooth paste and chill wrapped in cling film for 1 hour.
4. Halve the pastry and roll out on a floured surface.
5. Using a 10in. (25cm) flan case as a guide, cut out a circle from one piece to form a lid.
6. Use the other to line the flan case and prick the base.
7. Rest both in the fridge for 1 hour.
8. Make the filling by placing 12oz (350g) of the sugar and water in a thick-bottomed pan and stir over a low heat until the sugar is dissolved.
9. Increase the heat and allow the sugar to caramelise without stirring until it becomes a nut-brown colour.
10. Pour in the warmed cream (the caramel will react violently) and stir over a low heat until thoroughly amalgamated.
11. Increase the heat and cook for 2 minutes.
12. Off the heat, stir in the chopped walnut and cool to just warm.
13. Pour into the flan case.
14. Place the lid on top and press gently to seal.
15. Brush with egg white, sprinkle with caster sugar and cut a steam vent.
16. Place on a baking sheet in an oven preheated to 350°F/180°C/Gas Mark 4 and bake for about 40 minutes.
17. Cool before removing from the flan ring.

To serve the dish
Serve warm with whipped cream.

ABOUT THE SCOTTISH FOOD PROMS

THROUGHOUT this book you will have seen various references to the Scottish Food Proms. Held annually in Glasgow in April, this is a major festival of food and cooking. It was set up four years ago to promote the best of Scottish food and cooking.

Many of the chefs in this book have taken part in lectures, cookery demonstrations and dinners at the Scottish Food Proms. Every year, seven of Scotland's top chefs come together to cook the seven-course Gala Dinner at the Proms, which is widely recognised as the best culinary event in Scotland.

The week-long series of activities also includes sugarcraft, food photography, food illustration, food in the theatre, cake decoration, wine events, a conference for chefs and a conference for home economists. The event also organises the Scottish Food Awards.

The Scottish Food Proms has also been responsible for developing a major food-education initiative in Scottish schools. Every year, schools are invited to create Scottish Food Maps based on resource material published by the Scottish Food Proms. The maps are produced in a variety of media – including wood, hessian, cotton, polystyrene, and paper – and go on display as part of a major exhibition.

The Scottish Food Proms will shortly be launching the Scottish Food Proms Club, which will continue the activities of the Scottish Food Proms all year round and offer special dinners and cookery demonstrations as well as Scottish recipes to members.

If you would like more information on the Scottish Food Proms or any of its activities, please write to Scottish Food Proms, 16 St Brides Rd, Glasgow G43 2DU.

INDEX OF RECIPES